DISASTER RESPONSE

DISASTER RESPONSE

A *Handbook for*
Church Action

John C. Bush

HERALD PRESS
Scottdale, Pennsylvania
Kitchener, Ontario
1979

Library of Congress Cataloging in Publication Data

Bush, John C   1938-
    Disaster response.
    1. Church and disaster relief—United States.
2. Disaster relief—United States. 3. Disaster
relief—United States—Directories. I. Title.
HV554.4.B87   1979   361.5'0973   79-15090
ISBN 0-8361-1893-6

DISASTER RESPONSE: A HANDBOOK FOR CHURCH ACTION
Copyright © 1979 by Herald Press, Scottdale, Pennsylvania 15683
    Published simultaneously in Canada by Herald Press,
    Kitchener, Ontario N2G 4M5
Library of Congress Catalog Card Number: 79-15090
International Standard Book Number: 0-8361-1893-6
Printed in the United States of America
Design: Alice B. Shetler

15 14 13 12 11 10 9 8 7 6 5 4 3 2 1

This book is dedicated
to every person who gives
of himself/herself
to assist another
person in need.
May God bless you.

CONTENTS

A PRAYER*

Let us pray. . . .

Praise God from whom all blessings flow.

But, Lord, it's hard for us to accept adversity readily, to tolerate profound pain, and to understand why Fate seems so capricious, why some of us were devastated two weeks ago and others untouched. We couldn't help but be reminded of our relative importance and helplessness in the face of this greater power.

Most of us are again carrying on our "business as usual," yet in the middle of this busy day we interrupt our personal pursuits and pause. And we ponder. And we ask. . . .

What should we have learned from Your infinite wisdom? Are we fully open in our understanding? Or are we nearsighted and missing Your communication?

Did You mean to remind us of our oneness as human

---

*An invocation at the Topeka Rotary Club, June 23, 1966, following the tornado disaster. Reprinted in *Topeka Daily Capital, Rotopeka, Praying Hands, Journal of Pastoral Care,* and the *Congressional Record.*

beings struggling to survive, of the fallacy of being self-centered and too contented, of your proverb that "Pride goeth before destruction and an haughty spirit before a fall," of the necessity to think beyond ourselves and our immediate interests?

And in those brilliant, still moments after the storm had passed, did You mean to remind us of the brightness and glory that can follow adversity? Did You intend us to realize how we must help one another to achieve that goal, and understand the thought behind a Nigerian proverb which says, "When the right hand washes the left hand, the right hand becomes clean also."

As we consider these imponderables, will You please help us to understand how to accept and deal with the plight of those who have suffered and who are angry and resentful at being devastated or hurt. And assist us all in our responsibilities to lead others to bring forth new hope from our calamity.

We ask this, in Jesus' name. Amen.

W. Walter Menninger, MD
Senior Staff Psychiatrist
The Menninger Foundation

AUTHOR'S PREFACE

This is a "how to" book for church groups interested in developing a ministry to persons and communities affected by a disaster. It grew out of the experience of Kentucky Council of Churches' Interchurch Disaster Recovery Program and reflects that experience. Specifically, it emphasizes *models* of *interchurch*, or cooperative, responses to *natural* disasters. Let's start by looking at those three italicized words. They are important ones for understanding and using the material that follows.

Models. The idea of model building in reference to any aspect of the work of a church organization may sound strange. As used here, the idea has to do with a program or system of programs developed to aid in a specific mission which in turn may help in the development of other programs to provide similar ministries in the future.

Model building seeks to provide access to specific answers to the question, "What ought the church to do?"

The question makes certain assumptions. It assumes

that there is within the church a certain body of people who are *committed*—to Jesus Christ, to Christian faith, to the local church, to the idea of mission or ministry.

It also assumes that some of those people intend to express that commitment, and given the opportunity will do so.

It further assumes a willingness to plan specific ways to proceed so that the hope and faith of the people can be realized in concrete programs of action.

Such planning, then, leads to *mobilization* of the resources of the church/people (energy, skills, time, money, expertise), growing out of their Christian intention and commitment.

This is the approach to model building which informed the development of the system of programs which became the Kentucky Interchurch Disaster Recovery Program.

Interchurch Response. Some of the material in this book focuses on the work of a single congregation and what such a group can do. This is the exception, however, and should be viewed within the overall context of an interchurch, cooperative approach to disaster response. The interchurch approach does not attempt to gloss over the genuine differences that exist between various religious groups.

While theological and biblical reasons for church cooperation could be put forth, the most dynamic reasons for cooperation are purely pragmatic. Christians can get more done with the limited resources available if they work together in disaster situations. In a time of crisis, a Christian ministry of compassion and service which honors God above all can be the most meaningful

Christian witness. When God's people are drawn together by the Holy Spirit and engage together in showing His love, then the words of Scripture are fulfilled: "If you have love for one another, then everyone will know that you are my disciples" (John 13:35, TEV).

Natural Disaster. The experiences which led to development of this guidebook all arose from natural, rather than man-caused, disasters or catastrophic accidents. Specifically, the material reflects work done following the jumbo outbreak of tornadoes in 1974 and floods in 1975 and 1977 in Kentucky. The general outlines of how to organize and conduct a disaster response program are applicable to other kinds of disasters. However, other kinds of disasters present somewhat different psychological and theological problems and questions. Those involved in response to a catastrophic accident or a disaster caused by human frailty should be aware of these differences. Martha Wolfenstein underscores this point:

> I have spoken of natural catastrophes and the alternatives of the victims blaming their gods or blaming themselves or struggling to find some interpretation that is mutually exonerating. Where a disaster is man-made further possibilities and conflicts about assignment of blame enter in. In the war-time bombing of civilian populations the enemy is the obvious target for rage and indignation. But also blame may be directed against authorities on one's own side for not providing sufficient protection.

Christians generally have a theological framework within which to view those conceptions of evil which have their origin in persons. Shocking incidents such as

My Lai, political assassinations, corruption in government, corporate greed which saps the environment and endangers human life in order to wring the last farthing of profit—we have learned how to cope, though inadequately, with such human perversity. Our ethical and theological frameworks are accustomed to such questions of morality and human frailty.

Clearly in man-made disaster situations, and even in catastrophic accidents, we must deal with aspects of human sin, freedom, and responsibility. But in the case of natural disaster, the matter is different. Viewing the difference from a theological stance, one might assume that a different set of psychological questions arises within the same emotions (anger, guilt, fear) but from different circumstances. For example, anger with a person who has set forces in motion which caused one harm or pain is far more specific than anger which arises out of one's suffering from wind, rain, or lightning. One might logically assume that in the latter circumstances the resulting depression might be more persistent and the needed catharsis less readily experienced.

If the reader chooses to adapt the ideas and suggestions in this guidebook for denominational uses, or for use in some other disaster situation, much of this material will still be found useful. It is important, though, to realize that the model presupposed by the author is for a *cooperative* church response, and that his experience is with *natural* disasters. With this clearly in mind, we can now proceed to describe the work of the churches in such a ministry.

John C. Bush
Lexington, Kentucky

DISASTER RESPONSE

A Handbook for Church Action

1
BEING PREPARED: SOME PRIOR CONSIDERATIONS

"It won't happen here."

Such an assumption seems to characterize the view of most people about the possible destruction of their community by tornado, flood, hurricane, or earthquake. Even if it is recognized that some such catastrophe might happen, life is too full of other concerns for one to spend much time worrying about all the contingencies of our fragile existence on this earth.

But for some communities disaster will strike. The American National Red Cross recorded at least sixteen major disasters involving more than a million dollars each between 1967 and mid-1976, with scores of others involving substantial but lesser sums. Every state in the United States, without exception, has been affected by one or more major floods in the past thirty-five years.

It is appropriate, then, to give some attention to what might appropriately and feasibly be done by church leaders and organizations to be prepared for the contingencies of nature.

Local Congregations

Local churches are in a strategic position to provide certain kinds of advance preparation for their communities. The providential questions discussed elsewhere in this book certainly are related to the presence of congregations of God's people with local communities and neighborhoods as visible and lively expressions of the body of Christ in those places. The regular and continued teaching and nurturing work of the church can be a guiding influence which will prepare people to assume responsibility for a faith response in the context of difficulties and disasters. It is an important work of local congregations that they equip people to respond to the contingencies of life with hope rather than despair, and with creative work rather than only passivity or anxiety. These are among the practical outworkings of a doctrine of providence by which congregations of the faithful are prepared for ministry when disaster strikes.

There are other opportunities as well, which have to do with the presence of other church resources in the community. For example, those responsible for the policy regarding use of church facilities should give advance consideration to ways a surviving church building might serve a disaster-stricken community. Advance authorization for making the building available in the event of a severe emergency might be given to several key people, with the information provided to municipal and county officials.

As plans are made for new buildings and major renovation, advice should be sought from electric utilities and telephone communications consultants. In some circumstances, placing these service wires underground will substantially improve chances that service can be maintained through a storm. In Brandenburg, Kentucky, the United Methodist Church had taken this precaution only a few months prior to April 4, 1974. The church telephone was one of the few still functioning after the destruction of the town. The underground installation and the location of the church building in relation to grid lines and the path of the tornado were determining factors.

The slight additional expense of installing battery-operated floodlights in such buildings can provide a needed and welcomed resource both in the event of power failures and following a major disaster. Installation of a gasoline-powered generator for standby use can also provide an extra measure of preparedness.

What kinds of advance preparation can a local congregation and its leaders make to prepare it to minister effectively and appropriately to a disaster situation affecting its community? An answer must reflect the scope of the disaster, the prior and surviving resources of the congregation, and a realistic appraisal of the human capacities, abilities, and limitations of the pastoral and lay leadership.

Generally these ten advance preparations should be considered:

(1) Establish clear policies on the circumstances under which church facilities will be available to the public in the event of a community emergency.

(2) When building or major renovation is contemplated, consult with specialists on how to build in maximum feasible survivability for utilities and communication equipment.

(3) Consider installing alternate power supplies and lighting equipment.

(4) Inventory the skills and resources of people in your congregation who could render specific kinds of services needed in a disaster situation (see Form 1).

(5) Compile a list of the names, addresses, and phone numbers of amateur radio operators in the congregation or community and ask them to serve as channels of communication in the event of a disaster.

(6) Secure from denominational offices copies of any disaster response guidelines which they have prepared or adopted.

(7) Participate in area disaster preparedness meetings offered by the Red Cross or others, learning what existing disaster plans include and how churches can cooperate.

(8) Plan to channel immediate relief efforts through experienced groups such as Salvation Army or the Red Cross rather than establish a competing (and probably less efficient) church program.

(9) Anticipate the withdrawal of emergency relief agencies within 30 to 60 days and give careful consideration to longer term needs of the community.

(10) Recognize the limitations of one congregation alone, and be prepared to participate with others in a broader ecumenical effort.

City or Area

When an outbreak of storms covers most or all of a metropolitan area, county, or contiguous rural area, the most effective type of church response is an area-wide ecumenical effort. The Louisville-Jefferson County, Kentucky, and the Xenia, Ohio, disasters discussed in Chapter 3 are examples of such an approach. Similar ef-

SKILLS AND TALENTS

CHURCH INFORMATION

1. Denomination _____

2. Church _____

NAME and ADDRESS

3. Name _____

4. Address _____

5. City _____ 6. State_____ 7. Code _____

8. Home Phone _____ 9. Bus. Phone_____ 10. Ext.____

WHAT IS YOUR WORK?

11. Present _____

_____

12. Past _____

_____

_____

_____

13. Denominational Contact Person _____

14. I Speak   ☐ Spanish   ☐ German   ☐ Italian   ☐ Other

15. I Write   ☐ Spanish   ☐ German   ☐ Italian   ☐ Other

I HAVE ACCESS TO THE FOLLOWING:

16. Airplane—Seats: ☐ 2   ☐ 4   ☐ 6   ☐ More

17. Camper—Sleeps: ☐ 4   ☐ 6   ☐ More   ☐ Self-Contained

18. Truck—Type: ☐ Pickup   ☐ Dump   ☐ Flatbed   ☐ Van

19. Boat—Type: ☐ Inboard   ☐ Outboard

SKILLS AND TALENTS

	Novice	Journey man		Novice	Journey man
20. Carpentry	☐	☐	38. Radio/TV Repair	☐	☐
21. Farm Management	☐	☐	39. Gen. Office Work	☐	☐
22. Irrigation	☐	☐	40. Gen. Bldg. Repair	☐	☐
23. Animal Husbandry	☐	☐	41. Photographer	☐	☐
24. Agronomist	☐	☐	42. Poster Art	☐	☐
25. Cooking	☐	☐	43. Bus Driver	☐	☐
26. Pilot	☐	☐	44. Life Guard	☐	☐
27. Brick Mason	☐	☐	45. Music Instrument	☐	☐
28. Electrician	☐	☐	46. Counseling:	☐	☐
29. Plumber	☐	☐	Marital ☐ Youth ☐		Both ☐
30. Auto Mechanic	☐	☐	47. Rehabilitation: Prisoner ☐		
31. First Aid	☐	☐	Juvenile ☐		Both ☐
32. Legal	☐	☐	48. Veterinarian	☐	☐
33. Radio Operator	☐	☐	49. Architect	☐	☐
34. Printer	☐	☐	50. Medical Doctor	☐	☐
35. Appliance Repair	☐	☐	51. Nurse LPN ☐		RN ☐
36. Draftsman	☐	☐	52. Ordained Minister	☐	☐
37. Electronics	☐	☐	53. Alcoholics Work	☐	☐

54. Would you be interested in assisting in a project in a foreign country at your expense?   Yes ☐   No ☐

55. Does your work involve international travel?   Yes ☐   No ☐

56. Does your work involve state or national travel?   Yes ☐   No ☐

57. Would you be available for disaster relief with short notice?   Yes ☐   No ☐

COMMENTS

_____

_____

_____

_____

_____

NOTE: Providing this information in no way commits you to an activity, but rather, will help us to give you more complete information, from time to time, on projects suited to your abilities and interests.

forts were put forth in Omaha, Nebraska, in response to a savage tornado which struck there in May 1975. Based on their past experiences, Xenia Interfaith and the Omaha Disaster Task Force have established continuing emergency assistance agencies in their communities. In Louisville, the LAIODRP (Louisville Area Interchurch Organization Disaster Recovery Program) task force clearly saw its function as a temporary response to the yearlong recovery need, and disbanded itself upon completing its task.

These divergent approaches represent differing philosophies of organizing emergency recovery services, and suggest different approaches for advance preparation.

In general, the Kentucky experience has been directed toward the *ad hoc* approach based on meeting specific recovery objectives in response to carefully identified particular needs. In this context, the experience can inform advance preparation interests in areas without previous experience. One worthwhile idea is to involve a ministerial association or local council of churches in thinking together about a simple framework for a disaster recovery effort. This might include a tentative agreement among willing participants to work together in the event of a natural disaster in the area. A small working group might then become familiar with existing disaster plans for the area through the Red Cross, Civil Defense, or local government, identifying ways the churches might become involved.

The interchurch disaster preparedness plan could include a survey of church-owned facilities to identify in advance what services they might provide, such as emergency shelter, feeding, or communications (see Form 2).

In light of the importance of pastoral counseling and grief-crisis intervention, those involved in an advance plan might encourage pastors to undertake special study in this area or arrange seminars at theological seminaries or in cooperation with mental health associations.

This aspect of area-wide preparation will have at least two side benefits. First, it will provide the base for a crisis intervention program of almost any kind. Second, it will disburse new expertise over the metropolis or other area, upgrading overall pastoral service. It will help assure that sensitive counseling is available from some sector, no matter which specific areas are affected by the disaster. In addition, neighboring pastoral counselors are often helpful even for pastors who are affected along with the members of their congregations.

Lists of amateur radio operators, unemployed professionals such as nurses or social workers who could be called upon for volunteer assistance in an emergency, and ecumenical or denominational emergency assistance programs could be gathered in advance and circulated among all of the participating churches.

Obviously, one advantage to churches of an area giving some advance thought to a disaster plan is that they are then ready to help others nearby who may be affected. A small group could go into nearby affected areas to help the churches in the impact area assess the needs of their community and organize to meet them.

Keep in mind that Church World Service resources and technical assistance are available upon request by an area interchurch council or task force of cooperating churches serving the local area. Further, government and private agencies will find it easier to work with a cooperative effort of the churches.

CHURCH DISASTER PLAN

_____

(Name of Church)   (Address)

_____

(City)   (Code)   (Area Code)   (Number)

Description of church facilities:

a. Size of fellowship hall in square feet is _____

b. Seating capacity of fellowship hall is _____

c. Number of Sunday school rooms is _____

d. Seating capacity of the rooms combined is _____

e. Description of nursery facilities _____

_____

f. The total footage of rooms combined is _____

g. Size of dining area in square feet is _____

h. Description of restroom facilities and how many: _____

i. The kitchen facilities can prepare enough food for _____ people.

j. Description of kitchen facilities: _____

_____

k. Description of church-owned vehicles: _____

l. Other church facilities not mentioned are as follows: _____

_____

Person responsible for the administering of authority in case of a natural disaster:

_____

(Name and Title)   (Address)   (Code)   (Phone Number)

A Word of Caution

When any person or organization works in a disaster situation, a tremendous load of pain and problems will come their way. The evident and pressing needs will be staggering. The tendency is for persons to overwork, but this ultimately takes its toll.

Burnout is the word used to describe the fatigue often observed among disaster workers, both professional and volunteer. Watch for the signals that *burnout* is occurring, both in yourself and in persons with whom you work. There is no particular time schedule by which *burnout* works. Whenever it occurs, however, recognize it as a normal human response when the physical and emotional systems become overloaded.

Here are some of the signs that *burnout* is occurring:

(1) unusual irritability;
(2) oversensitivity to the comments or actions of others;
(3) increased hyperactivity;
(4) depression;
(5) radical changes in sleeping or eating habits;
(6) obvious discouragement for unusually long or frequent periods of time;
(7) lowering of energy or motivation level;
(8) increased and excessive criticism of others;
(9) unrelenting weariness or unusual nervousness;
(10) dramatic drop in efficiency and the ability to get things done.

Such signs are ways the human body and mind have of telling you that you or your associates are overworking, pushing yourselves beyond acceptable limits. As valuable as the contribution each person makes is to the total recovery effort, each of us must also recognize that the work of recovery does not depend upon us alone.

There are things which can be done about *burnout*. Leaders should plan for ways to assist staff and volunteers in a regular debriefing process. Talking about the problems one is encountering can help.

Here are some other suggestions:

—Time for prayer, meditation, and devotions (private and with others) can be important.

—Recreation. Physical playful activity and regular nonwork exercise can provide a great release for the bodily tensions that build up.

Time off. Getting away from the project for a day, a week, or month might be the best approach.

—Reduced involvement with especially tension-creating tasks might be needed.

—Consider opportunities to do many different kinds of things—physical labor, advocacy casework, counseling—rather than spending all of your time at only one kind of task.

Burnout affects different people differently. It comes to some people earlier than the others. It will not go away by itself. It must be planned for, discussed openly, watched for, and dealt with.

2

HOW PEOPLE REACT
TO DISASTER

A disaster neither begins nor ends once the danger is past. Even for those who survive with life, limb, and property intact, the experience begins before impact and continues long thereafter. The disaster is an intrusion into the total life of an individual—emotional, physical, and spiritual—which requires time to assimilate.

A number of individuals have outlined the normal sequence of reaction to a disaster situation. Common to all of these suggestions is the idea of a pre-disaster, or threat, stage. This threat stage includes two substages within it: (1) a period of denial, when the threat is not admitted; and (2) a period of anticipation, when the threat is acknowledged. We shall now consider the predisaster stage and its denial and anticipation substages.

Denial: The Threat Not Admitted
Life is filled with dangers and with constant potential

for disaster of one sort or another. Even so common an occurrence as walking or driving to the grocery store is not without hazard. A child's game can suddenly become fraught with danger. At any time or place one may contract some dread disease, or suffer a heart attack or stroke. But who can worry about all such contingencies? We must recognize that some of the dangers of life are quite remote. Only the unhealthy mind and spirit spends a great deal of time worrying about all the terrible things that might happen. Still, when danger does actually threaten, this normal attitude of denial can continue to function and become itself an unhealthy attitude.

Myths of Community Immunity. It is not unusual to find various stories abroad in communities across North America indicating that a particular community is immune to tornadoes, floods, or earthquakes. The tornado which devastated a portion of Topeka, Kansas, in 1964 passed over a small knoll outside the city known as Burdette's Mound. Local folklore, attributed to early Indian settlers of the area, indicated that Burdette's Mound protected Topeka from tornadoes. In some communities such folk wisdom is given more acceptance than contemporary weather forecasts, and whole communities depend upon some kind of magical protection against disasters.

The feeling of immunity, especially from a danger which has never been experienced before, is often very strong. Following a tornado in San Angelo, Texas, one victim said, "They warned us, but I didn't think it could happen here." A resident of Kansas City, Missouri, who experienced the 1961 flood there, admitted having heard flood warnings on the radio, but said, "I thought they were talking about the Kansas side. I thought we would be all right."

Sometimes whole communities continue with this sense of immunity right up until the moment the danger is upon them.

Belief in Personal Immunity. Individuals tend to deny any threat or danger to themselves. They may say something like, "It can't happen here, but even if it does it can't happen to me." Even when it is recognized that, for example, a tornado is about to strike a community, many persons refuse to believe that it can affect them.

This strong belief in personal immunity tends to be most pronounced in situations where the individual can do nothing as a precaution. For example, if a person does not have a basement or storm cellar and doesn't know anyone who has such a facility, that person is likely to take a ruggedly independent attitude of self-immunity. The idea of immunity also tends to be reinforced when taking a precaution requires some great inconvenience. For example, evacuating oneself and belongings from an area threatened by a flood represents considerable inconvenience and requires a great deal of energy and effort. The result is that people in flood areas often feel a sense of personal immunity. They will want to "wait and see what is going to happen," in the continuing belief that the water will not get any higher. Such individuals will often want to stay to protect property, disbelieving that any threat to their life or safety exists. In the impact phase, however, this attitude is reversed, for when a threat to life actually materializes, concern for property is greatly reduced.

The sense of personal immunity is particularly enforced by the North American positive self-image, the take charge attitude and "Yankee ingenuity." Communities recently affected by floods are often filled with people who refuse to believe that another flood can happen, or that if it does, the flood waters will not reach their property again. These communities often depend upon new dikes or higher flood walls that have been built. They are disillusioned to discover that their trust in technology is sometimes misplaced.

Consequences of Denial. Denial of any possible danger to one's community or self can have continuing personal and emotional consequences. Obviously, it can lead people to place themselves and their property in grave danger by refusing to heed warnings. In a more lasting sense, it has been observed that more emotional disturbance exists in the post disaster phase among those who have denied the threat of real danger than among those who have accepted the threat and taken precautionary action. It seems that anticipation of the threat has an inoculating effect and reduces the likelihood that the person will be emotionally overwhelmed by the experience.

Those who have denied any danger until it is too late often have more intense fear of a repetition of disaster than do those who have recognized the danger. Persons who admit no sense of danger to themselves are often shattered when danger actually materializes. Those who admit the possibility of harm are more prepared to accept the risks and therefore tend to come through the experience more intact emotionally.

The fact that it is important for people to know what to expect in a disaster situation underscores the value of

FLOODS/FLASH FLOODS, 1955-1971

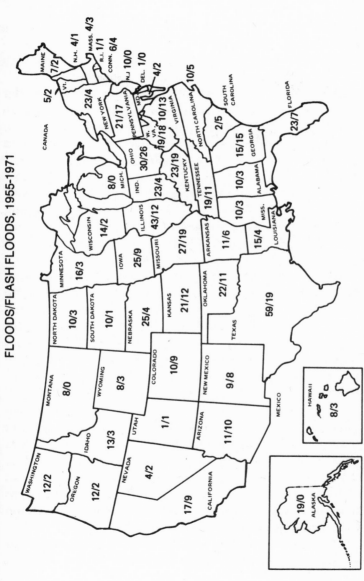

Number of Floods and Flash Floods in Which American Red Cross Assistance Was Given, 1955, 1971 (data from American National Red Cross).

preventive or precautionary planning in the church's ministry to disaster situations.

Anticipation: The Threat Admitted

We turn now to consider the situation where the existence of a threat is admitted. In some instances that admission will not be made until the disaster has already occurred. In other cases the admission may come just ahead of impact—as, for example, when high winds and battering waves portend the arrival of a hurricane. During this period advance precautionary measures are put into effect. Characteristically, during this phase people become intensely alert to indications of the threat. In tornado country, people will begin watching the clouds and taking weather forecast warnings more seriously.

It is not unusual in this setting for an air of excitement to prevail, perhaps an almost holiday atmosphere. In flood-threatened areas it is not unusual for crowds to gather near the riverbank and watch the water rise. In areas threatened by hurricanes, neighbors sometimes make a party out of putting up the window covers and making preparations to protect life and property.

There are a number of popular myths about what to anticipate in a disaster situation. It is often thought, for example, that if the people are told about the severity of the threat that there will be mass panic, with people running through the streets crying and screaming. The fact is that masses of people do not flee in panic in a disaster. The literature on the subject abounds with references to how quiet the people are, to the calmness with which they go about the task of making the best of the situation. Evacuations come, when they are called for, in ways that are relatively quiet and orderly. The visions of panic are

TORNADO INCIDENCE BY STATES, 1953-1970

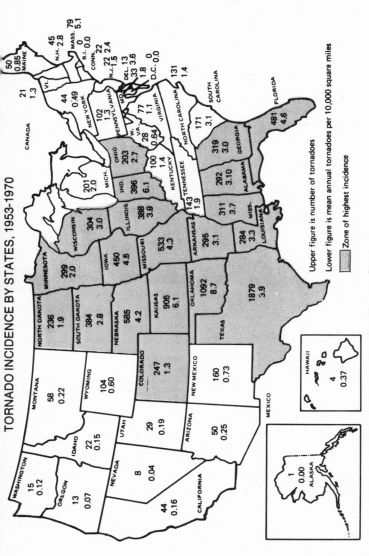

Upper figure is number of tornadoes

Lower figure is mean annual tornadoes per 10,000 square miles

▨ Zone of highest incidence

Tornado Incidence by States, 1953-1970–(National Weather Service).

more related to the psychological needs of those who anticipate disaster than they are to the actual behavior of people in a disaster situation.

There is also a myth that emotional illness increases immediately following a disaster. However, there has been no evidence to indicate an increase in long-term mental illness attributable to disasters. There are indicators of emotional stress which can be anticipated, such as increases in alcoholism, rises in the number of divorces, and an increased death rate among the elderly. However, there is no reason to fear an outbreak of mass insanity or a dramatic increase in permanent mental illness in connection with a disaster.

Planners who anticipate disaster behavior always include the expectation of looting in their plans. The fact is that looting on a large scale rarely occurs in a disaster situation. In most disasters rumors will surface that looting has occurred, but arrest or conviction for looting in a disaster situation is rare. Apparently people need to expect the worst from others in a disaster situation. Fortunately, the worst rarely materializes.

This has been a discussion of the threat stage of disaster response. The second major stage identified by most students of disaster behavior is the impact stage.

Impact

The initial response to disaster for most people, obviously, is fear. It is not unusual for people to become alarmed about the impending danger. That alarm intensifies when an individual is with a group of persons. Even in a group situation panic is rare, however. The literature abounds with descriptions of individuals in restaurants or bars taking shelter together, showing concern for others in the group, and giving level-headed advice.

For most people, however, the experience of a disaster is a solitary one shared only by members of the household. Sometimes, in that solitude, alarm is not highly aroused or intensified.

When the immediate impact is past there is a tendency for each person or group of persons to think that only they have been affected. A victim at Brandenburg, Kentucky, reportedly said, "Why doesn't somebody come to help us? Can't they see that everything has blown away?" In part, this mistaken impression can be attributed to the fact that most of us have only had experience with disturbances that affect us or our households, such as sickness or an ailing furnance or a problem with the plumbing. Our first thoughts, therefore, relate to a limited problem. For some people, however, this individualistic interpretation is a part of the desire to deny the terror of what has happened. This is illustrated by one person who had heard flood warnings, but still told himself that the water he saw on the floor had been spilled there. '

Another misinterpretation of the circumstance common to disaster victims is what may be called an "illusion of centrality." The person mistakenly believes that, while others have been affected, the force of the disaster has affected him more than others. The victim tends to think that he or his household has been the central point of destruction with the effects of the disaster radiating out from that point of reference.

Certainly the experience of a disaster requires the concentration of a great deal of emotional energy on oneself. The simple act of surviving, protecting one's loved ones, and assuring oneself that one has survived after the impact understandably account for an illusion of centrality. This illusion is, perhaps, the other side of the pre-impact assumption about one's own invulnerability. Prior to the impact it is not unusual, as we have noted, for people to feel that something may happen to others but not to oneself. When the impact has occurred there is a sudden reversal of the perceived immunity. The individual knows that he is not immune but assumes that the rest of the community has remained intact and that others will soon come to his aid.

This leads to the next stage of assimilating the scope of the disaster. Characteristically this involves a feeling of loneliness or of having been abandoned. Friends and neighbors whom one has expected to provide comfort and assistance do not appear because they also are involved with freeing themselves from the effects of the disaster. In a short time another change may also occur in feelings. During the impact, individuals often comment on the strength of the storm and their feeling of weakness in relation to it. But as they recognize the scope of the damage, individuals often report a return of a feeling of their own strength. They no longer feel hopeless, but turn to help others whom they often perceive as being "worse off" than themselves. The initial fear that the disaster may have been aimed particularly at one individual disappears.

A part of assimilating what has happened sometimes results in an increase in rumors about the scope of the disaster, with victims often reporting that the damage is far greater than is actually the case. The reported loss of life in the immediate period after impact will be greatly exaggerated. Rumors will circulate within the community about the death of particular persons who may

MAJOR DISASTERS BY STATES, 1961-1970

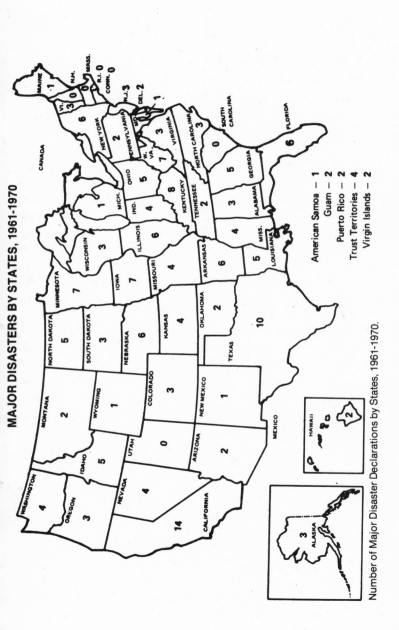

American Samoa — 1
Guam — 2
Puerto Rico — 2
Trust Territories — 4
Virgin Islands — 2

Number of Major Disaster Declarations by States, 1961-1970.

have been either greatly loved or particularly disliked within the community.

Disaster victims often recount an intense increase in their feelings of love for others and their feeling that others love them and are being particularly good and helpful in the post-impact phase. The idea of community solidarity following a disaster has frequently been noted and studied with interest.

Immediately following a disaster there is a tremendous output of energy, both by survivors and by outsiders who come to their assistance. Many persons work exceptionally hard and put in long hours rendering whatever service they can. The North American tendency toward frantic activity, "doing something," can be useful for rescue workers, but it does not necessarily guarantee that the work being done is highly efficient. Disaster literature is full of references to people who "don't know what to do" to be helpful. Certainly, facilities are limited. People are upset. And many are incapacitated by "disaster syndrome," characterized by depression and inability to be active.

This inefficient activity is often noted particularly among professional people. For instance, physicians trying to be useful may be thwarted by an inability to concentrate on one or a few tasks or patients, as they rush from place to place rendering a little assistance to many persons. One minister who was outside the impact area of the Topeka storm put it this way:

> When it was past and I heard what had happened, I put on my clerical garb and headed toward the area which had been hit first. . . . I went to the shelter in the school. . . . Everybody wanted to help but nobody knew what to do.

. . . Most high level professional functions seemed to evaporate in the emergency and it was personally difficult to let them go and just work. My clerical garb didn't provide much help, except to identify me as a person who could be addressed in a mass of people. That's how I got to work with a pad a pencil registering people. People weren't able to talk expressively. . . . They seemed to be relieved to have somebody write down their name and note that they were alright.

During this period of intense activity another phenomenon is often discovered—the feeling of a marked separateness between survivors in the impact zone and those who come in from the outside after the event. The outsider/survivor dichotomy sometimes becomes intense and may be expressed at a slightly later stage as anger and resentment toward outsiders, even if the outsider has been helpful. At least partially, this is because the survivors do not recognize the significance of themselves to outsiders. The outsider has a need to establish contact with people who may need help. But the survivors are busy with the task of readjusting to their experiences and what has happened to their world. They fail to recognize how significant they are to others.

Further, the intense activity after impact may also be a means of escaping the harshness of what has happened. The processes which are psychologically defined as "mourning and symbolic detachment" are not immediately available. Those processes are often supressed by the frantic activity which may be seen as almost an attempt to undo the terrible damage which has come upon them. The grief and mourning processes seem to begin about the third or fourth day following the event, and that appears to be the best time for a pastoral ministry to begin, utilizing the basic methods which a pastor or counselor would use with persons experiencing bereavement from the death of a loved one.

This leads to a slight digression. Often during this phase of a disaster situation, individuals think of human loss primarily in terms of loss of life. If a house or tree was destroyed, but persons escaped alive, we often say, "Well, at least you didn't lose your life." That is not entirely true, and is not always a helpful response. When a man who is now 70 years old loses his family pictures; when an elderly woman loses a rag doll which was her dead daughter's last valued possession; when a couple loses an oak tree which Dad and his son planted sixty years ago—and the son is now old and near death; then these people did lose a part of their lives. It is not helpful to them when we fail to see the loss from their perspective.

It is well for those who minister in a disaster situation to ask, "What does it do to a community when half of it is gone within a space of five minutes? What does it do to a school or a church when half of the people lose everything and the other half nothing?"

A great deal of guilt settles on people who escaped without serious loss when friends or relatives suffer so much. That guilt is as much a part of the lasting effect of a disaster as any of the physical losses which might also be incurred.

The Aftermath

A disaster is not over when the immediate danger has past. As we have just seen, even among those who survive a disaster without great personal loss, there are continuing consequences. Of course, the greater the degree to which one was personally affected by the disaster, the more time or emotional energy it will take to assimilate these consequences.

A part of this assimilation process is the need to relive, again and again, the painful and frightening experience. This is done by talking about what happened, by telling the story in detail over and over again to others, by comparing experiences with others who suffered through it, and sometimes by dreaming about the experience. There is great variation in the ways individuals respond, however, and for some the trauma will have been so unbearable that they will attempt to repress it completely. They will, in fact, not remember portions of the experience. They may not be able to talk about it. They may seek to avoid all reminders of the disaster, sometimes going to great lengths to do this.

A staff person with the Kentucky statewide disaster organization visited an affluent community about two years after the tornado there almost obliterated portions of the community. There were almost no signs that the catastrophe had ever occurred. Mature trees had been brought in and planted to replace the damaged ones. In a door-to-door survey the interviewer found only one family still living in the area who had been in the tornado. That person attributed most of the moves to the painful memories of the tornado which had killed or injured several persons.

Some persons who survive a disaster cannot talk about it, do not want to hear about it, and avoid the site on which it occurred at all cost.

At the other end of the spectrum are those who live almost constantly with the memory of the experience without ever seeming to exhaust their feelings of anxiety or distress. Such persons can't seem to get over the experience, and continue to devote a great amount of thought and energy to it.

In spite of these diverse ways of assimilating disaster trauma, however, it is generally accepted that a reliving or retelling of painful experiences is one means by which the grief or anxiety can be overcome. Some observers believe that those who do not have an opportunity to anticipate the possibility of the disaster have a more difficult time overcoming the emotional aftermath of the event. The longer one has to prepare for a possible disaster, the easier it seems to be to overcome the lingering emotional effects.

We have said that some of the emotional elements at work following a disaster are similar to the processes of grief after the death of a loved one. The acceptance of loss requires a time of mourning. This is accomplished by bringing to memory those fond associations with the person or object lost and through that process, in effect, saying good-bye to each and detaching oneself from it. If this process is avoided or short-circuited, those elements of distress will come back at some future time and will have to be dealt with later. It is important, therefore, for ministers especially (but for any person who works as a volunteer) to recognize this need and to plan for its incorporation into the work done immediately following a disaster.

We have noted the situation in one community where those who experienced a disaster moved away. Students of disasters indicate that this is not a typical reaction, however. Most often, while they continue to feel some apprehension about doing so, people move back to the general area where they lived prior to the disaster. In

EARTHQUAKE-RISK ZONES IN THE UNITED STATES

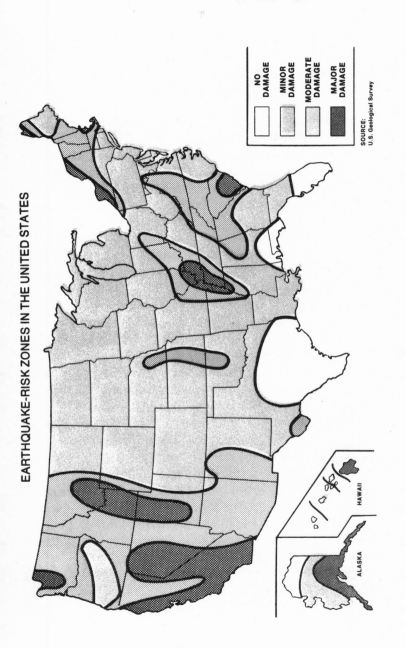

NO DAMAGE
MINOR DAMAGE
MODERATE DAMAGE
MAJOR DAMAGE

ALASKA

HAWAII

SOURCE:
U.S. Geological Survey

North America people from towns affected by tornadoes, hurricanes, floods, and earthquakes are inclined to build new homes in the vicinity of the ones lost or damaged. This going back seems to be an emotional response growing out of strong attachments to the place which has been home. Those attachments apparently are more easily broken by a voluntary decision to move elsewhere than by disasterous circumstances beyond one's own control. This could be seen as a part of the grief process involving the need to master the anxiety, guilt, or grief suffered in the disaster.

Generally, those who move away are those who have been unsuccessful in mastering the pain and anxiety by reliving it and who wish instead to escape it and repress it. It seems likely that these people will have continuing emotional problems as a result of the disaster.

We have already noted that feelings of great love for others often emerge immediately following the disaster. These feelings are a part of a general upsurge in good will and helpfulness which is sometimes called "post-disaster utopia." Distinctions between races and social classes are blurred and help is shared as needed rather than on the basis of other considerations which might be important outside the disaster context. A great sense of respect for those who suffered through the disaster arises among outsiders or those who were near but not directly in the disaster scene. Survivors are idolized as martyrs or heroes. Their courage is often complimented. The victims themselves express great appreciation for the goodness and helpfulness of others.

Unfortunately such a circumstance cannot be long maintained and this post-disaster utopia degenerates quickly. People who have given of their time, energy, or resources without counting the cost begin to express regret for their generosity. Suspicion arises and people criticize those who have accepted "too much." Rumors begin to circulate about how some have gotten rich off the emergency assistance agencies. Stories surface about people who lost nothing receiving large amounts of aid. Worry emerges about whether one has received "one's share" of the help available, rather than seeing others as being worse off than oneself.

The first sign that the post-disaster utopia is over often is seen in the critical attitude toward emergency assistance agencies and organizations.

Individuals who at the height of the emergency willingly accepted food or clothing now begin to refuse assistance. They will often do this on the grounds that "there may be someone who needs it worse than I do." But, in fact, by refusing they are putting distance between themselves and "those who need help." Individuals who accept help are often seen as "undeserving" by others at this stage. It is likely that they will be seen as either not needing or not deserving assistance.

On the other hand, those who do not qualify for private or governmental assistance often begin to express hostility because they did not get their fair share. This is a complete shift from the immediate post-impact tendency to sincerely disavow one's own need and to recognize the needs of others.

During several disasters in the 1976-77 period, emergency food stamps were available to any disaster victim. This was a recognition that following a flood or tornado, for example, no matter how wealthy a person might be their resources are not immediately available for food purchases. In the post-utopia period, great hostility arose over those provisions as well as over efforts by the Red Cross and other agencies to distribute food and other assistance to people without stiff requirements being met.

At the same time, hostility also emerges in the post-utopia period toward the procedures which assistance agencies use to evaluate the circumstances of applicants. Many seem to feel that their losses are not adequately recognized. The cold procedures of bureaucratic agencies come under great criticism. The real victims become torn between their genuine need for help, on the one hand, and the North American ideal of individualism and self-sufficiency on the other, which makes people resent both the offer and the need to accept assistance.

They become wrapped up in a complicated reaction in which people express reluctance to accept help and at the same time engage in secret or open competition to see who can get the most.

This tendency also makes relief agencies victims of the disaster. Those who administer federal programs are accused of all kinds of mismanagement. Relief agency officials are charged with using their supplies to their own advantage. Political leaders are blamed for using relief supplies for their political gain. Relief agencies are suspected of being concerned too much with who gets the credit for what is done, and being in competition with other organizations. The local business community resents the goods distributed by relief agencies, in the belief that this in some way takes away from their business. The weather service will be criticized for not giving adequate warning of the pending storm.

The decline of the post-disaster utopia is inevitable. It is one sure sign that life is returning to normal.

3
MODELS FOR DISASTER MINISTRIES

The social scale of a disaster should be the guide for determining the level on which a church response is developed. When a single community or metropolitan area is affected, that is the scale on which to organize an overall long-term disaster response. When the effect is felt over a number of counties, then the response should be appropriate to that area. When a disaster affects all or the major part of a region, then the churches should respond to the situation at that scale.

What follows is a series of models which have been used by local churches and by groups of churches to respond at several levels. The experiences described are those of particular groups involved with specific disasters. It is not intended that the reader attempt to reproduce any one or more of these in a specific situation. Rather, these models should be read as sources of ideas which may be of use in a disaster ministry where you live.

A Metropolitan Area

Louisville, Kentucky. During the first week after April 3, 1974, church leaders in Louisville-Jefferson County, Kentucky, met to coordinate their responses to the disaster and to plan for meeting future needs of disaster victims. The result was a task force related to Louisville Area Interchurch Organization for Service (LAIOS). Many Louisville area churches became involved in the recovery effort by offering facilities, supplies, and volunteer labor.

Church groups throughout the storm-damaged area responded impressively, spontaneously, compassionately, and with strong grassroots leadership for the metropolitan area program.

The group organizing the disaster program consisted of representatives from regional denominational offices, neighborhood ministerial groups, religious disaster relief organizations (such as MDS and Salvation Army), and ecumenical neighborhood ministries throughout the affected urban area.

There were 29 persons on the board, which remained a fairly stable group through the seven months of program operation. Technical assistance in setting up the organization was provided through Church World Service. The group called itself "Louisville Area Interchurch Organization Disaster Recovery Program (LAIODRP).

Initial funding came in the form of a grant from Church World Service. The resources offered by CWS are described in more detail later in this book. (See pages 153-158.)

It was decided that the most appropriate source of funds for the disaster ministry would be the various levels of denominational support. Some denominations raise money for such projects directly from local churches. Others contribute to a national fund, from which money is granted to local interchurch or denominational disaster programs.

Consultant services and outside volunteer assistance came from the Christian Reformed Church World Relief Committee, Mennonite Disaster Service, and Church World Service.

The Louisville board identified six purposes for itself. These were:

(1) to coordinate volunteers recruited by churches and religious organizations, both locally and out-of-state;

(2) to maintain contact with persons in the tornado affected areas of the metropolitan area regarding their recovery needs;

(3) to advocate for residents with governmental and other agencies providing services and assistance;

(4) to secure and provide material and financial assistance to needful households, utilizing funds given to LAIODRP and related sources;

(5) to provide pastoral counseling, utilizing the existing services of Interfaith Counseling Center; and

(6) to make staff available for other direct services as needed.

Arrangements were made for a group of students from Kent School of Social Work at the University of Louisville to work with the program in making and maintaining contact with persons in affected neighborhoods. This proved to be a highly effective aspect of the program. Months after the tornado, the students encountered people who still needed to ventilate their feelings about the storm and its effect on families. They found several parents who wished to discuss the adjustment problems their children were having with fear of common weather conditions such as wind and rain.

The program provided direct financial assistance in the form of small grants to alleviate some of the more pressing financial problems faced by families who had not received (or were not eligible for) federal disaster assistance. These funds covered such items as pressing rebuilding or repair costs, temporary housing, rental deposits, purchase of furniture, business expenses, and clothing.

An important element in the Louisville-Jefferson County program was "end-of-the-block" neighborhood meetings, conducted by LAIODRP staff and staff members from Interfaith Counseling Service, a church-sponsored pastoral care center. One purpose of these neighborhood meetings was to help neighbors support each other in the recovery effort, and to discover emotional needs and offer appropriate resources. They also channeled questions, complaints, and requests to appropriate agencies and allowed "debriefing" functions of the recovery process to occur in a positive manner. The major purpose of this particular program was to facilitate mutual support of persons within the smallest neighborhood unit in tornado-affected parts of the urban area.

Xenia, Ohio. The same jumbo outbreak of tornadoes which affected Kentucky and led to the Louisville program also affected Xenia, Ohio. The twister cut through the city, from suburbs to the urban core and out the other side, with a damage path varying from a quarter to a half-mile wide.

Shortly after the disaster Protestant, Roman Catholic,

and Jewish religious leaders formed an agency to minister to the physical, spiritual, and emotional needs of the Xenia community which became known as the Xenia Area Inter-Faith Council. It was based upon a model developed at Rapid City, South Dakota, and at Wilkes-Barre, Pennsylvania, when religious leaders mobilized to assist flood victims in those communities.

Xenia Inter-Faith was an independent ecumenical agency which received funds totaling about $816,000 from ten Christian bodies. It developed coordinative relationships with the Christian Reformed World Relief Committee and with Metropolitan Churches United of Dayton.

The strong focus of Xenia Inter-Faith was upon advocacy. The service aspect of the program was organized in three response areas, called advocacy units.

Field Advocates were recruited and trained to interview victims and make referrals to other agencies for assistance. Those not eligible for assistance elsewhere could receive direct grants from Xenia Inter-Faith to meet critical needs. This element served 1,600 families. Volunteers came from the Christian Reformed World Relief Committee, Mennonite Disaster Service, and other churches and communities.

These persons provided direct services to families, and do not appear to have been "advocates" in the strict meaning of that word.

Institutional Advocates were related to federal and state disaster aid programs as these were instituted. Their task was to assist families and individuals in relating to available programs and to make the programs responsive to the needs of victims.

Community Advocates served as volunteers in rebuilding and repairing homes and businesses. Again, their function was not strictly advocacy. Xenia Inter-Faith coordinated volunteer labor which produced about $1.5 million worth of labor.

Some Observations. Because attention has been focused here on the interfaith model of disaster response, this seems an appropriate place for some observations on this approach to church response. The interfaith concept has been widely publicized and replicated in a number of disaster situations. It is a good basic model which is widely advocated by such agencies as the Christian Reformed Church World Relief Committee.

When appropriate to the actual situation, the name "Interfaith" is a good one. In using it, however, one should be aware that it means an organization or group which includes more than one religion—not just different Christian denominations. The denominations are all of the same faith—Christian. If the disaster response group includes the Jewish community, Mormons, Buddhists, or persons from any religions other than Christian, then the name "Interfaith" is appropriate. A group which is composed of Protestant, Catholic, Evangelical, and Orthodox communities is not interfaith, though it is interchurch. If a name similar to "Interfaith" is desired, why not "Interchurch"?

Any response entity, regardless of what it is called, should belong to the local community. Its board should be composed of persons from within the affected area, along with consultants from outside as needed. The goal of the recovery effort is to enable the community to return to normal and to regain its appropriate degree of autonomy. If this is to happen, the community must be in control of the recovery process as it develops there.

And finally, the organization put together to respond to the disaster must see itself from the beginning as temporary, and as having disaster recovery as its specific objective. It must be recognized that this task will ultimately be completed. Recovery will occur. When it does, the organization should not seek to perpetuate itself as an additional social service agency. It should recognize its achievements and put itself out of business with dignity and celebration. If the churches then wish to bring some other form of organization into being with other objectives, then this will be a strong added resource in the community as a result of the disaster recovery effort. But the new group should be really *new*.

I recognize that disbanding a group which has suffered and worked together through a difficult task is not easy. It is an emotional event in itself. Organizations die hard. The tendency is toward perpetuation. The decision that the recovery effort is finished and that the organization has completed its work must be made consciously and in good faith. It is another sign that the disaster is over. A public service of thanksgiving and praise would be an appropriate ending for such a group.

Statewide Models

Kentucky Interchurch. According to the director of Mennonite Disaster Service, the Kentucky Interchurch Disaster Recovery Program was the first ecumenical statewide disaster effort attached to a state council of churches. During the month following the storms of April 3 and 4, 1974, which devastated thirty-three Kentucky counties, the Kentucky Council of Churches entered into consultation with denominational officials

and representatives of state and federal agencies to as-
certain directions and needs for a statewide church disaster response.

Early in the planning a distinction was made between
emergency *relief* and disaster *recovery.* Relief was seen
as helping affected persons acquire the basic necessities
to continue living. Temporary shelter, a supply of clothing, emergency food supplies, medical attention, and the
ability to communicate with distant or temporarily lost
relatives are among the pressing needs of people in a
disaster situation. In planning its program, Kentucky
Council of Churches identified three phases in dealing
with disaster needs. The first is *crisis aid:* Initial digging
out, feeding, sheltering, comforting, and otherwise caring for victims of the disaster. The second is *basic relief:*
Getting people into temporary housing, establishing
contact with relatives, cleaning up the rubble, assuring
that clothing and food needs are met while families and
persons get themselves pulled together again. The third
and longest phase is *recovery.* While crisis aid may
continue for twenty-four to forty-eight hours and basic
relief for thirty to sixty days, recovery is likely to continue
for a year or more.

This third phase, recovery, was determined to be the
objective of the Kentucky Interchurch Disaster Recovery
Program, a cooperative effort of the churches of
Kentucky to provide long-term caring and assistance to
people affected by natural disaster in the state. Technical
advice and assistance in planning and establishing the
program was provided through Church World Service,
by the national director for Mennonite Disaster Service,
and by a consultant from the United Methodist Committee on Relief.

THE KENTUCKY INTERCHURCH DISASTER RECOVERY PROGRAM

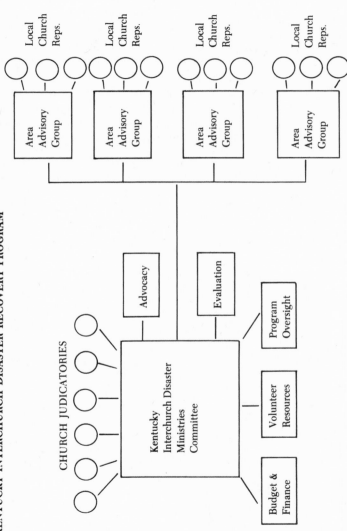

A committee of the executive board of the council served as the steering committee for the project. This committee made a tour of most of the thirty-three Kentucky counties affected by the series of tornadoes. They talked with pastors, church leaders, public officials, and disaster victims in many Kentucky communities attempting to assess the needs which the churches could help meet. Following these field visits, a day was spent assimilating the data which had been picked up on the tour and outlining a general program design with five major emphases:

(1) Crisis counseling to persons and families, providing and supporting a ministry to the emotional and spiritual needs of those who have suffered loss of loved ones, homes, property, or community.

(2) Warehousing and distribution of furnishings, housewares, clothing, and food needs by families as they rebuild and return to normal.

(3) Direct assistance, especially to the poor and elderly who sometimes lack the ability to relate to bureaucratic processes, or who because of pride do not seek the assistance they need.

(4) Support of and a referral source for local church persons, who often find unique and very personal ways to serve persons and families.

(5) Person-to-person assistance and advocacy, especially in rural and isolated areas where people who need assistance are often difficult to locate and may not have direct access to existing assistance resources.

A program narrative describing this project and the resources needed to implement it was written and sent to denominational relief agencies through Church World

Service. The proposal generated sufficient cash to support the program and allowed the project to provide volunteer assistance, goods, services, and grants worth about $500,000 over a one-year period. The resource mobilization aspect of the project was combined with the Louisville program under a joint funding agreement. The organizational structure is illustrated in the diagram on page 59. A job description for the program director is found in the appendix (page 169).

At least 1,100 families were assisted, either through the direct grants and services of the program or through advocacy cases affected by work with state government in its implementation of the Federal Disaster Act.

Person-to-person advocacy with individual clients who applied for the Individual and Family Grants Program (Section 408) and other federal disaster programs produced a significant number of favorable grant eligibility determinations, and the reconsideration of grants which had been awarded in unrealistically low amounts. Such reconsideration advocated by the interchurch program almost always resulted in the significant increase in the amount of the Section 408 grant awarded to a disaster victim. For instance, in one dramatic case, an original grant award of $700 was increased upon appeal to more than $3,600.

A Clergy Crisis Conference was planned and conducted as part of the project. The primary purpose of the conference was to assist pastors from stricken areas to "debrief," to express and understand their own emotions and thoughts. The secondary purpose was to provide a supportive framework for the counseling ministry of these pastors as they dealt with the emotional and spiritual problems of their people.

In a retreat setting, training and support was provided to clergy from disaster-affected communities. The purpose was to assist local pastors in understanding the special grief and guilt processes present in the lives of persons in their communities following the disaster, and to equip pastors in dealing with those processes in the lives of their people, as well as in their own lives. In addition there was theological discussion on the "Theology of Chance and Providence."

The conference resource team was a professor of pastoral care at Southern Baptist Theological Seminary, a Christian psychiatrist, and a theologian.

Texas Conference of Churches. In February 1976, the Texas Conference of Churches (TCC) announced formation of a program of response to disaster as a permanent part of its structure. The Texas plan arose from an experience in Lubbock following the disaster there on May 11, 1970, which resulted in devastation and disorganization.

Supported by some alert Lubbock clergy, the Federal Office of Emergency Preparedness set up a central disaster headquarters and coordinated all the activities of the federal government under one roof. This approach proved valid as a way of coordinating activities, especially the services made available to disaster victims. This one-stop center approach has become a model for subsequent federally declared disasters.

The TCC sought and received approval to continue to work cooperatively with federal programs in Texas disasters. The TCC disaster team goes into the disaster area with the federal team, establishes a joint headquarters with them, has immediate access to the first and best assessments of the devastation, and establishes a linkage for local church officials with incoming groups, both governmental and volunteer.

The TCC sends in a standby disaster team of persons experienced in disaster work and familiar with other responding units, which is prepared to initiate the TCC program as needed.

The Texas strategy builds upon the idea of "one-step help" for disaster victims. TCC plans to serve as a switchboard for volunteers and volunteer agencies to meet a variety of needs which fall between the gaps of other helping agencies.

Eight "Helping Activities" are identified in the TCC disaster response program:

(1) Making church buildings and facilities in stricken areas available as disaster centers, or shelters;

(2) Providing a central clearinghouse of volunteer workers to be mobilized from local churches and civic organizations throughout Texas, including an Adopt-a-Family program, linking unaffected residents with a stricken family for direct support and assistance;

(3) Giving priority field attention to low-income and minority groups who may be reluctant to go to the disaster centers, using volunteer aides and caseworkers;

(4) Providing a Community Information Center, or rumor response center, to give reliable information to the community;

(5) Providing secretarial personnel to manage a central filing system on each stricken family, recording the extent of damage suffered, new location, future plans, services needed, and services received;

(6) Giving immediate volunteer and financial assistance;

(7) Setting up a nonprofit emergency corporation to

receive, hold, and disburse financial assistance for disaster victims;

(8) Facilitating the extraordinary ecumenical cooperation possible in the disaster situation, both within and from outside the affected area.

Multi-County Regional Model

Central Mississippi. In June 1971 an eighteen-county area of central Mississippi was devastated by a series of tornadoes. The hardest hit victims included a large number of low-income farm worker families at Iverness in Sunflower County.

The tornadoes destroyed the small tin-roofed homes of the farm workers. Substandard housing was the norm for low-income people in the storm-damaged area.

The Department of Housing and Urban Development provided a federal response with emergency mobile home units for temporary housing. Clearly the need was for new housing that would be decent, safe, and sanitary.

A disaster team of carpenters was sent by the Church of the Brethren to live and work in Inverness for three months. Several homes and a church were rebuilt. Affected families assisted the carpenters, cutting costs, and learning valuable building skills.

Assistance was sought from the Rural Housing Alliance (RHA), a Washington-based nonprofit housing organization. RHA sent a housing specialist to work with community groups to form a locally controlled nonprofit housing corporation. After reviewing housing assistance which was then available to the rural poor, the decision was made to try a self-help program.

In a self-help housing program, families work together to build their own homes. It is a direct application of the old-fashioned barn-raising still practiced by the Amish and the Mennonites. Families provide the necessary labor, assisting each other in building their homes, and a Farmers Home Administration (FHA) housing loan covers materials, land, and subcontracted work.

Groups of six to ten families locate land, select housing plans, obtain cost estimates, and apply individually for FHA loans. While the loans are being processed, the families engage in a study course on home ownership responsibilities, construction techniques, work schedules, tool use, fire insurance, taxes, interior decorating, and home maintenance.

When the loans come through, construction begins with guidance from a skilled supervisor. Each family works an average of twenty hours a week while the houses are being built. The work is scheduled so as to avoid interrupting regular family employment.

Some of the technical work such as wiring and plumbing may be subcontracted. The rest of the work is done by members of the families. Construction takes six to twelve months, depending on how many houses are involved.

Delta Housing Development Corp., the local organization set up to operate the self-help program, is a nonprofit Mississippi corporation. The corporation has continued long beyond the disaster recovery period to deal with the housing needs of low-income families in the Mississippi Delta region.

Congregational Model

Topeka, Kansas. After a disastrous tornado struck Topeka, Kansas, on June 8, 1966, Westminster Presbyterian Church devised a "Tornado Counselor Plan" as a ministry to members of the congregation affected by the storm. The special significance of this model is that it is congregationally based, pastorally oriented, and directed toward long-term recovery.

More than fifty Westminster families were hit by Tornado Topeka. Some homes were a total loss, with others slightly damaged, and many in between. Subsequent heavy rains aggravated the situation. The immediate emergency had been met. Everyone had food, clothing, and shelter.

But what about the long-range problem? What about permanent housing, insurance, leases, transportation? Many people were facing the reality that life must go on and the gigantic problems of getting back to "normal" living.

The board of deacons of Westminster Presbyterian acted to set up a "Tornado Counseling Plan" to give long-range assistance to Westminster victims on a personal and continuing basis. The plan assigned a Tornado Counselor to each affected family in the congregation. On a one-to-one basis, the counselor was responsible for determining the family's needs, informing the family of assistance and resources available, and helping them secure whatever help was needed.

Some families, because of their wide acquaintances and resources, needed little help. Others required financial assistance, some to a large extent. Some needed advice on all kinds of problems since they were not experienced in operating in crisis situations. Others received all the help they needed from relatives or friends.

The counselor was provided with whatever pertinent information the church had gathered from pastoral visits, phone calls, or secondary sources. The counselor was responsible to carry through on his own and to solve all the problems he could. When he got stuck, he could ask for help through the church office.

The pastor and deacons enlisted the volunteer efforts of "experts" in the congregation to assist counselors as needed.

The counselors were thought of as advisers, helpers, or catalysts. They were the only official representative of the church assigned to their family.

The counselor was released from his assignment when he determined that he had given the family all the long-range help they needed or that the family had sufficient resources to make further help unnecessary.

Complicating Factors. People's feelings are of the utmost importance in this kind of ministry. The following material was included in the advance kit provided to each counselor:

> *Facts* and *feelings* may not match at all. The counselor may see that the family needs lots of help, but they may say they do not. On the other hand, the family may, with no apparent provocation, express anger at the counselor or the church. Why? It is important for the counselor to have some knowledge of what happens to people in and following a disaster. The following should be helpful:
>
> (1) There is often the strong need to *relive* the experience, by *talking and talking* about what happened. Occasionally, however, you may find the opposite, the desire to deny all thought of the experience, a steadfast refusal to allude to what happened at all, even when appropriate and necessary in order to make plans for the future.
>
> (2) There may be other reactions such as *sleeplessness;*

inattention to what is going on now; inability to center down to planning; fear of a recurrance of the disaster. This latter often leads to rushing out to buy transistor radios, lights, extra supplies. This results in the neglect of present plans and needs.

(3) People are likely to feel a sense of failure after a disaster, as if somehow they should have been able to ward off the tornado, or keep it from striking their home. Likewise, we who escape damage may experience feelings of "success," wanting somehow to congratulate ourselves on not being hurt. Obviously, these feelings are irrational, but nonetheless they are *real.*

(4) Early response to property damage is to *minimize* it. "What's a house? We have our lives!" *Later,* this feeling gradually changes and the property damage is felt to be much more significant.

(5) There is a nearly universal insistence that "There is no need to help *me* personally; I'm all right." This is coupled with, "We were lucky." Even when members of the family are killed, and homes demolished, there is a tendency to think of others as *worse off.*

(6) Early in the aftermath, there is a good feeling about others, that everyone has been so helpful. The end of this stage is usually signaled by criticism of *agencies* or *institutions* that have helped (the Red Cross, Salvation Army, National Guard and police, the churches, and the like). The later reaction includes feelings of anger, depression, and bitterness.

(7) Persons who were in the destroyed property at the time of the disaster seem to adjust sooner to the loss than those who were away and came back to view their damaged or destroyed home.

Your reactions as a counselor to these possible reactions are vital. It is important to *understand* and *accept* them as "natural" under the circumstances.

(1) If you meet with a stricken family in the early stages of

their reaction, they may minimize the whole thing, tell you they need no help, that they were lucky, that everyone has been wonderful. You can't expect them to ask for much help or tell you directly about their needs. The best approach is to ask them what happened to them, listen to their reliving of the event, and pay special attention to clues they drop which help you understand their needs. After they have talked, you can ask specific questions [see the counselor's checklist on page 70], even though they may protest that they are fine. Note problems you see, without pressing them about them, with the idea you will return later to determine if these matters need attention. Don't count on one visit to settle anything. Your second visit will convince them of your intent to help long-range, and will help you to see the difference in attitude as time goes on.

(2) If you find the family in the later stages of their reaction, you can expect to feel a little uncomfortable with their attitude (see No. 6 above). They will not be angry with you personally (though it may seem that way), nor even necessarily angry with helping agencies. The anger is frustration and hurt at what has happened. You can't get angry at a tornado, so you get angry at people, or the church, or perhaps with God! At this stage, they may despair of getting back on their feet. Concentrate on specific needs. Do not let them throw themselves completely on you or the church. You are not a cure-all and cannot right everything that is wrong.

Say: Let me see if I can help you find the name of an attorney to assist you with your settlement; or, Let me help you find some pots and pans for your kitchen; or, Let's see if we can find a place for you to live.

Do not say: Don't you worry about a thing. We'll take care of everything.

Assignments, Records, and Reports. Individual assignments were made to counselors by the pastors, on the basis of the most urgently known needs. A card file on each victim was maintained in the church office. Duplicates were given to the counselors on an assignment card.

Counselors were urged to keep the church office informed from time to time on what they were doing. As phone calls about the affected families arrived in the church office, they were referred to the counselors for coordination efforts. Interested parties were told that the counselor was in charge officially for the church so far as a particular family was concerned. This kept the responsibility for individual families coordinated through the counselor and also kept the church office from being swamped coordinating these efforts.

Counselors were asked to record carefully and accurately all their contacts with their assigned family. In this way if a counselor's personal situation changed to prevent follow-through, the family could be easily reassigned to another counselor with adequate information on what had been done.

Each counselor's kit contained the counselor's checklist printed below to look for other concerns.

Here is a list of questions you might have in your mind as you visit with your family:

(1) Have contacts been made with insurance, bank, and time payment creditors?

(2) Have arrangements been made for appraisal, repair work?

(3) Have legal requirements been checked on leases, liability coverage, claim procedures, and the like?

(4) Medical expenses? Are they settled? Hospitals will likely bill for emergency treatment later where records are available.

(5) Is there a need for temporary housing? Semi-long-range housing? Permanent?

(6) Are necessities available for employment? Tools, eyeglasses, clothing, transportation, and the like?

(7) Household necessities. Are cooking, housekeeping equipment, and other supplies available on a semi-long-range basis? What about pots and pans, refrigeration, stoves, baby items, dishes, and the like?

(8) Other aid available. Has contact with the family been established by the Red Cross, Salvation Army, and other agencies? What help (specifically) is forthcoming? Money? Clothing? Furniture? You need specifics here, *not* generalities.

(9) Are kids provided for? Toys, bikes, swings, bathing suits? Is there need for nursery care over the long-haul? Semi-long-range? Temporary? Is the mother looking for work to supplement income?

(10) The freeway proposal, while as yet indefinite, is being taken seriously. Keep an eye on developments here which might affect the family's plans to rebuild or make major repairs.

(11) What about immunization shots for tetanus for those working on wrecked sites?

(12) Does counselor know attorneys, insurance men, loan people, contractors who might assist if counselor gets stuck? If not, the church office can help suggest such persons.

Of course the test of the plan came as counselors began to call on families. A number of the families were already getting back on their feet, but even in such situations, the counselors often felt that it was helpful to these families to know that the church was interested.

Many kinds of aid were offered—transportation to the doctor, assistance in obtaining estimates, getting housewares together, taking the kids to the park for a day while parents cleaned. Direct money gifts were rarely accepted by the families, however. Even though the church had set up a fund, they discovered that the people were unwilling to use it. One man said, "I *give* to the church, I don't *take* from it." The congregation then decided to use the fund to make up the pledges to the church of those hit by the tornado so they could put their money to use in their own recovery. In the end, however, there was no drop in giving to the church. In spite of their losses, the members paid their pledges to the church.

Some people who were in the tornado found it difficult to accept help. Some were embarrassed and even angry about what the church was doing. The word "victim" in the church literature offended some. The counselor's calls produced some signals to the pastor that special attention was needed by particular families. For the most part, however, people seemed genuinely grateful that the church was aware of their needs, sensitive to their feelings, and trying to minister to them in practical ways which did not lower their own self-esteem.

Getting Organized: Some General Guidelines for Local Interchurch Response

Church World Service (CWS) has prepared the following guidelines to assist local groups in setting up an interchurch response to meet human needs in a disaster situation.

(1) The local ecumenical agency, a prominent church official, or a designee should contact local government authority (mayor and county commissioners) and Red Cross to determine the severity of the disaster and offer churches support.

(2) Report the situation, local capability, and *a plan of action* immediately to the CWS Domestic Disaster Office, New Windsor, Maryland (301) 635-6464 or TWX number (710) 862-9190. This will trigger alerting denominations of the disaster and possible request for national assistance. CWS material aid will be discussed.

(3) If the situation warrants, call an emergency meeting of your ecumenical group. Invite representatives of all local churches and area denominational leaders to attend.

(4) Since the disaster is a *community responsibility* and local churches will assist in the recovery, the following agenda is suggested:

a. Invocation

b. Welcome and introductions

c. Report on situation and action of local government—mayor, county commissioner, civil defense director, sheriff, and the like.

d. Report of survey, shelters, needs of people, and action taken—Red Cross official.

e. Report of services being rendered by other voluntary organizations active in disaster—Salvation Army, Volunteers of America, denominations, and the like.

f. Ask churches to prepare a list of resources to bring to the next meeting.

(5) Appoint a steering committee responsible to set up the structure necessary to assume the long-term recovery job. This could be a subcommittee of the ecumenical agency with other local denominations added or a separate group independent of the agency convening the meeting. It may be incorporated as a separate group and may be representative of the community. In either case, it should remain the churches' disaster response as a vital part of the total recovery efforts of the community.

(6) If local leadership has had the CWS-certified orientation and have the organizational and training kit, they

should be equipped to start action. If not, request the CWS Domestic Disaster Coordinator's office to recommend an organizer and/or counselors (from denominations with this expertise such as Christian Reformed World Relief Committee) to assist in getting started. They will train your people to do the job . . . not do it for you.

(7) The local ecumenical body should encourage fund raising within the churches in affected areas immediately, as soon as the disaster is defined. Local church efforts should be conducted in conjunction with national denominational practices.

(8) Assign a liaison person as soon as possible to the Red Cross, the Federal Government Disaster Agency, Civil Defense, and the local government.

(9) Appoint a person to serve as liaison for the local ecumenical agency to inform local and national media (including press, radio, TV, civic clubs, local government, Chamber of Commerce, and the like) of objectives and services rendered.

(10) Always keep the CWS Domestic Disaster Coordinator's office informed so the office may advise denominations outside the disaster area what you are doing.

(11) Plan regular meetings. If the recovery response unit is separate from the original ecumenical group, then there should be regular reports to the ecumenical group.

(12) At the first meeting of task force, have the Federal Government Disaster Agency and Red Cross report regarding resources.

Helpful Hints from Other Communities
Having Gone Through This Same Experience

It is essential to have a representative from all participating churches on the churches' disaster response board. Should the number exceed ten, an operations or executive committee should be appointed with authority to act for the board when not in session. This becomes the administrative unit to the director, if the task is going to be large enough to employ a director.

Arrange for early contacts with local government, Chamber of Commerce, civic clubs, and special interest groups to explain *local* plans for long-term assistance on the part of churches as their part of the total community effort. While recovery is a local government responsibility, most local officials welcome other agencies assisting people, as their big job is restoring streets, buildings, utilities, and the like.

Keep liaison not only with Red Cross and Federal government but also with local or state welfare departments, health departments, institutions, employment offices, Social Security, and the like. It is well to have one person designated to act as the liaison officer for your group to explain the role of the advocate to these agencies.

If you need assistance in training advocates, do not hesitate to request experienced trainers in this field through CWS Domestic Disaster Coordinator's office. The same is true if you need experienced organizers to assist you in setting up your organization.

If needed, all volunteer workers should have tetanus shots. All career and professional workers should have typhoid shots (and all others if the germ is in area).

NOTE: The federal agency that coordinates all government and private agencies has asked CWS to arrange through its channels to furnish volunteers (advocates) to assist applicants in filling out the mass of government forms, and to continue with the family through the emergency period. Your organization should be prepared to meet this request. Government will assist in the training of these volunteers. This is a continuing need—to emphasize the partnership between the government and the private sector to effect the best possible service to the disaster victim.—Reprinted by permission of Church World Service.

4
A THEOLOGICAL POSTSCRIPT

Why This Ministry?

An important assumption lurks in the title of this book. The assumption is that a natural and human disaster which requires a response is legitimately a matter for churchly concern.

Is this assumption correct? What possible relationship can there be between the work of the church and the phenomena of tornadoes, floods, or earthquakes? To ask such a question involves a discussion of church as servant community, redemptive community, and prophetic community.

These three aspects of the churchly nature are ways of understanding what the church is all about. The emphasis must be upon what the church is before one can understand what the church does or should do. Much of the literature produced since the mid-1960s on the theology of involvement errs at this point. It places emphasis upon the *doings* of the church rather than emphasizing its *being*. We must recognize that the primary element of the churches' work can be discovered by looking at the nature of the church rather than by examining the nature of the problems it addresses itself to.

Servant Community. The primary New Testament image of the church is that of *faithful servant*. The central theme of the ministry of Jesus was to call His disciples to participate in His mission through love and service. While natural human communities are characterized by competition and self-interest, the community of the faithful servant "esteems the other better than himself," Christians are called to participate in a new life within a new creation, where the barriers of class, culture, race, prestige, and human condition are transcended. The servant people are called to be present within the world.

If the church is to be the servant of God's mission, it must, like Christ, be sensitive to the points of disjunction in the world. It must be so structured that it focuses the obedience of the Christian community at these points of need, bringing the healing resources of Christ to bear in such a way that His forgiveness and love become bridges across the chasms of separation. It would seem that this task obliges Christians to use fully the "secular" means which God offers us in the world—means by which we can discern the points of need and match them with the responsive structures of Christian community.

Redemptive Community. The church of Jesus Christ, a servant community, is also a redemptive community. The vocation of God's people is to show forth, in both

word and deed, the work of reconciliation already
achieved in Christ.

"I believe in God the Father Almighty, Maker of
heaven and earth; and in Jesus Christ His only Son, our
Lord. . . ."

When Christians begin to say what they believe, using
words of this ancient creed, they are affirming that the
world and everything in it is created and governed by the
power of God, the Father of our Lord Jesus Christ. The
statement is not a scientific one about the origins of the
physical universe so much as it is a spiritual affirmation
about the foundation of life.

Creative force is the essence of life, a force which humankind discovers within itself and observes in the world
round about. Humans cannot live without being affected
by the gigantic forces of creativity at work in the world.

In ordinary times and under ordinary circumstances,
people of faith have no difficulty saying the familiar
words. By experience we know and believe that we live in
an ordered cosmos, one which provides for our physical
needs as surely as night follows day, season upon season,
year after year. The orderly pattern of nature provides
structure for our day. Even though few of us now earn
our livelihood from the soil, we are aware of the ways in
which soil, moisture, temperature, sun, moon, season,
nutrients, and wind combine with labor, mechanical ingenuity, and research to produce food and fiber.

At the same time, our separation from so many of nature's functions—birth, death, planting, and harvest—
also contribute to our sense of alienation from nature.
We must take to our cars and travel through traffic,
smog, and urban sprawl to drive through a few miles of
"open country" and "see nature" through the glare-

proof glass of our air-conditioned vehicle listening all the while to electronic music in quadraphonic sound.

Along this pastoral route we may pass the skeletal remains of an old oak or elm, a battered barn upon the hillside, or signs of a stream recently swollen beyond its banks by rainfall. In an occasional field we may see cornstalks rustling in the breeze, reminders of a drought or flood that made the crop not worth the effort to harvest. On our drive, we will have observed nature. We will not have known it.

But there are times when nature refuses to stay at arm's length. Sometimes it will not be manipulated by our elaborate machines and the devices by which we think to control our environment. Occasionally nature comes crashing through all of our defenses and confronts us with the naked power of wind and driving rain, of twisting and grinding forces which transform our familiar surroundings into grim reminders of gigantic battlefields.

In such times, the world especially needs a community of faith, a redemptive community of God's people who are reconciled to God and sent into the world as His reconciling community. This community, the church universal, is given a message of reconciliation and a mission of healing all the divisions which separate people from God and from one another. The suffering of Christ makes the church sensitive to the sufferings of people, so that she is able to see the face of her Lord in the faces of people in need. The suffering and crucifixion of Jesus of Nazareth make known God's judgment upon the inhumanity which people show to one another and upon our involvement in continuing injustice. It is precisely in the power of a risen Christ, and the hope of His coming, that the church proclaims the promise of a renewal for all people and a victory over even the most terrible tragedies of life.

Prophetic Community. The *prophetic* nature of the church is the third important aspect of the being of the church. In many places, Scripture describes the church as the "first-fruits" or "earnest" of the ultimate transformation in which "the kingdoms of this world become the kingdoms of our God and of his Christ." Though the church often fails to live up to its vocation, shielding from sight the "signs" of the kingdom of God, it is still true that this community of baptized faithful has within its life the very embodiment of hope.

Faced with a disaster which confronts the souls of people with the serious question of "why," the Christian prophet speaks from a stance of faith. We speak of a God who acts with and for people, and we seek to plumb the depths of His will. This awareness of the divine is expressed in a sense of the awe and ambiguity of life in this world. That sense of awe is brought to consciousness in the renewal and insight shared within the prophetic community which bears witness to Jesus Christ. This awareness of the divine is both historical and personal. It is at once real and illusive, reassuring and threatening, present and absent, known and uncomprehended.

This prophetic community, which is the church of Jesus Christ, is composed of people whose redemption is still a reality which is waited and hoped for, as well as one which belongs to the present time. (See Romans 8:22-25.) This community of faith is intended by its Lord to be an exemplary community and a challenge to the world around it. Its purpose is not to dominate but to serve; not to express pride, but humility; not to hate but to demonstrate love.

This prophetic community dreams of a golden age when the natural antagonisms of this world will no longer exist; when the lion and the lamb will lie down together; when joy and harmony will fill all of nature; and when all people will live at peace with the world and with each other.

Of particular interest are the melancholy words of the Apostle Paul in Romans 8:19-22 (a passage powerfully interpretated by Paul Tillich in his sermon, "Nature, Also, Mourns for a Lost Good"):

> Even the Creation waits with eager longing for the sons of God to be revealed. For creation was not rendered futile by its own choice, but by the will of Him who thus made it subject, the hope being that creation as well as man would one day be freed from its thraldom to decay and gain the glorious freedom of God's children. To this day we know, the entire creation sighs and throbs with pain. Romans 8:19-22.

The prophetic community of Jesus Christ is in a good position to ask whether our contemporary seclusion from nature has so enclosed us in our sense of human superiority that we are incapable of hearing these words of the apostle. We, the dominators of the natural order, like all merciless rulers, have so insulated ourselves from that which we have subjected that we cannot hear the sighs and throbs, the groaning after salvation of which Paul speaks. Do we dare admit the truth—that, for all of our technologies and philosophies, we too are a part of the natural order of things? Can we hide always from the reality that God has made this world to be an interdependent world and therefore we are a part of the world of nature as well as humankind?

Only because we have succeeded in convincing ourselves that our superiority removes us from the rest of creation are we able to wreck the devastation upon land, sea, and air which characterizes our "civilized" age, and to do so in the name of progress. By our violence and greed, nature is "rendered futile," so that all of creation has fallen victim to our sin, brokenness, pride, and rebellion. Nature, as well as we ourselves, needs to be "freed from its thraldom to decay and gain the glorious freedom of God's children."

Created together in glory, humankind and the natural world belong together in tragedy and in salvation, until the old heaven and the old earth shall pass away and the new be born. Humankind, meant to fulfill and bring order to the whole world, is itself empty and disordered. Being broken, how can we bring wholeness to the world? We can neither fulfill nor order nature—not our own nature, and not the nature which surrounds us.

But the same Paul who gave us this strange and melancholy insight has also given us the picture of "the new Adam." "As in Adam all die, even so in Christ shall all be made alive." In Christ the forces of death, separation, and tragedy are overcome, not only for us but also in the universe. The salvation and victory over decay and death which we know in Jesus Christ is for all of creation.

What a magnificent message of prophecy and hope this is which rests with a prophetic community. Within this context, the church as prophetic community is especially equipped to understand and interpret the crucial questions of faith which are raised by the disaster experience. The prophet can help the church respond to the contingencies of life with faith, hope, and creative aggressiveness, knowing that the universe is not neutral in its destiny.

The affirmation that history and nature are converging toward a spiritual destiny is an essentially prophetic affirmation. The church of Jesus Christ lives its life and witness open to the future, which is God's creation and gift, knowing that the future is not merely an extension of the past but is an opening to new events and to newness of life.

Being and Doing

At this point we may return to form a link between *being* and *doing*. From this understanding of the church, we can affirm Christian responsibility in continuing the work of creation. It is precisely in a world where suffering falls upon people unequally and haphazardly that true kindness, compassion, and unselfishness are possible. We must be conscious of God's presence in His church, shaping it, forming its nature, and working through its people to define both its being and its doing, so that in times of trial, temptation, and adversity the church is prepared for a ministry of servitude, redemption, and prophecy.

This ministry is summarized beautifully in a leaflet which is distributed by Mennonite volunteers in a disaster-affected community. The folder bears the title, "Why We Are Here."

> *Bear ye one another's burdens, and so fulfill the law of Christ. . . . Thou shalt love the Lord thy God with all thy heart . . . and thy neighbor as thyself.—The Bible*

We may be strangers to you but you are our neighbors. We cannot fully understand your loss but we want to share your burden.

We wish to follow Christ and His teaching in all our living. We consider anyone in need our neighbor. When disaster strikes we desire to give assistance as we are able.

God sent Jesus into this world of distress and sin because He understands and wants to help those who are in need. As Christian people we want to share this love with you by helping you and reminding you that Christ died to redeem each of us.

If we can be of further assistance, whether physical or spiritual, please feel free to call on any of our volunteers.

5
DIRECTORY OF RESOURCES

Resources available to persons and groups working toward a church response to a natural disaster situation in the United States and Canada are varied. Many resources, including published materials, are available from governmental units, private and quasi-private agencies, and church bodies. General information is provided here regarding all of these resource categories, and specific information is included for some. Knowing of these resources will help religious groups function more effectively within the context of a total disaster recovery effort.

Governmental Resources

Clearly, government has certain fundamental responsibilities following a natural disaster. At its several levels, government should act to protect life and property, restore public services, protect public health and welfare, and administer certain tax-funded assistance programs.

Such action ordinarily originates at the local (municipal or county) level, with assistance being sought from state (civil defense, state police, public health, and other state services) and, perhaps, federal agencies.

Responsibility for coordinating governmental action is determined by the scope of the disaster. A merely local catastrophe is likely to be handled entirely from the office of the mayor or top-level county official. If a disaster affects a significant portion of a state, primary responsibility for coordination will probably be lodged with the office of the governor or a state agency designated by the governor. In most states, an Office of Emergency Preparedness, attached to the civil defense or State National Guard, will be designated with a member of the governor's staff providing liaison.

Many federal assistance programs can be implemented only after the President of the United States, on request from the governor, declares an area a major disaster area.

A chart of "Emergency Individual Disaster Services," which illustrates the scope of federal assistance, appears on pages 90 and 91.

Special Note About the New Federal Emergency Management Agency

As this book was being prepared, the President of the United States announced a reorganization of the federal emergency management and assistance programs, many of which are described in the section on governmental resources.

The plan merges five agencies from the Departments of Defense, Commerce, Housing & Urban Development, and General Services Administration into one new agency. It creates the Federal Emergency Management Agency, whose director reports directly to the President.

The five agencies being merged into the new FEMA are

(1) Defense Civil Preparedness Agency (from the Department of Defense).
(2) Federal Disaster Assistance Administration (from HUD);
(3) Federal Preparedness Agency (from GSA);
(4) National Fire Prevention and Control Administration (from Commerce);
(5) Federal Insurance Administration (from HUD)

The plan for the new agency calls for ten regional offices, which are the same as those indicated in the descriptions that follow regarding the Federal Disaster Assistance Administration (FDAA).

The reorganization does not abolish any functions or programs. It simply consolidates responsibility for implementing and overseeing most of the programs described in the pages that follow into a single agency, the Federal Emergency Management Agency.

Because implementation of the reorganization is still in process, it has not been possible to edit all the material in the govermental resources section to reflect the changes.

EMERGENCY INDIVIDUAL ASSISTANCE SOURCES

If You Need ... Emergency Assistance	You Can Get ...	From These Agencies and Sources
Food	Food stamps Food packages Meals and surplus food	State Welfare Department Red Cross Salvation Army
Clothing	Personal effects Free replacement of clothing	Small Business Administration Red Cross Salvation Army
Housing or home furnishings	Temporary shelter Temporary housing Furniture and appliances	Red Cross Dept. of Housing and Urban Dev. Salvation Army, Red Cross
Medical care	Help in getting medical care Emergency medical care and health service	Red Cross Public Health Service
Assistance for homeowners: Home repair or reconstruction	Loans for home repair Insurance or mortgage to fix home Help to pay for home Work assistance in rebuilding	Small Business Administration Dept. of Housing and Urban Dev. Dept. of Housing and Urban Dev. Local Charitable Orgnizations
Assistance for business owners Business repair or maintenance	Loans to repair or replace your business	Small Business Administration

Assistance for farm owners		
Rural home owners farm operation	Loans to repair or replace farm buildings	Farmers Home Administration
	Help for farmers	Farmers Home Administration
	Help in getting feed for livestock	Agricultural Stabilization and Conservation Service
General Assistance		
Social Security, welfare, or veterans services	Help in locating relatives	Red Cross and Salvation Army
	Social Security or Veterans benefits	Social Security Administration and Veterans Administration
Legal assistance	Legal advice	Young Lawyer's Section–OEP
Employment advice	Job help	State Employment Service
	Compensation	
Income tax assistance	Tax help for disaster victims	Internal Revenue Service
Property Clean-up	Help clean-up property	Local governmental units
Official information	General public information and assistance	Office of Emergency Preparedness
Federal Assistance to States and Localities		
	Set up emergency health and sanitation procedures	Public Health Service
	Establish public health controls	Food and Drug Administration
	Help in clean-up operations	Dept. of Defense/Corps of Engineers
	Restore roads and bridges	Department of Transportation
	Search and rescue	Coast Guard
	Repair flood control works	Corps of Engineers

Summary of Assistance to Individuals from Federal Emergency Management Agency

One of the most important objectives after any disaster is to inform individuals of the assistance available to them and to assist them in obtaining all the aid to which they are entitled. Information is disseminated by FEMA through radio, television, newspapers, and mass distribution of pamphlets outlining available aid programs.

To make it easier for individuals to get information and obtain the help available from various federal agencies, FEMA establishes one or more Disaster Assistance Centers in the disaster area. Representatives of federal agencies, local governments, private relief agencies, and other organizations which can provide assistance or counseling are available to register and advise disaster victims. These "one-stop" centers are kept in operation as long as required by the situation. In addition, mobile teams may be sent to assist persons in areas not easily accessible to the centralized Disaster Assistance Centers.

A presidential declaration of a major disaster makes a broad range of assistance available to individual victims of the disaster. This help may include:

Temporary housing for disaster victims whose homes are uninhabitable until other housing resources are available. No rental is charged during the first twelve months of occupancy;

Minimum essential repairs to owner-occupied residences in lieu of other types of temporary housing resources, so that families can return quickly to their damaged homes;

Temporary assistance with mortgage or rental payments for persons faced with loss of their residences because of disaster-created financial hardship for a period not to exceed twelve months;

Disaster unemployment assistance and job placement assistance for those unemployed as a result of a major disaster;

Disaster loans to individuals, businesses, and farmers for refinancing, repair, rehabilitation, or replacement of damaged real and personal property not fully covered by insurance;

Agricultural assistance, including technical assistance; payments of up to 80 percent of the cost to eligible farmers who perform emergency conservation measures on farmland damaged by the disaster; and donation of federally owned feed grain for commingled livestock and herd preservation;

Distribution of food coupons to eligible disaster victims;

Individual and family grants of up to $5,000 to meet disaster-related necessary expenses or serious needs of those adversely affected by a major disaster when they are unable to meet such expenses or needs through other programs or other means;

Legal services to low-income families and individuals;

Consumer counseling and assistance in obtaining insurance benefits;

Crisis counseling and referrals to appropriate mental health agencies to relieve disaster caused mental health problems;

Social Security assistance for recipients or survivors, such as death or disability benefits or monthly payments; and

Veterans' assistance, such as death benefits, pensions, insurance settlements, and adjustments to home mortgages held by the Veterans Administration if a VA-insured home has been damaged.

This summary is taken from a "Program Guide" prepared by the Federal Disaster Assistance Administration, April 1977.

U.S. DEPARTMENT OF HOUSING AND URBAN DEVELOPMENT
Federal Disaster Assistance Administration

Region 1
(Connecticut, Maine, Rhode Island, Massachusetts, New Hampshire, Vermont)
JFK Federal Bldg., Rm. 2003L
Boston, MA 02203
(617) 223-4270

Region 2
(New Jersey, New York, Puerto Rico, Virgin Islands)
26 Federal Plaza, Rm. 1349
New York, NY 10007
(212) 264-8980

Region 3
(Delaware, District of Columbia, Maryland, Pennsylvania, West Virginia, Virginia)
2 Penn Center Plaza, Ste., 1426
Philadelphia, PA 19102
(215) 597-9416

Region 4
(Alabama, Canal Zone, Florida, Georgia, Kentucky, Mississippi, North Carolina, South Carolina, Tennessee)
1375 Peachtree St., NW, Ste. 750
Atlanta, GA 30309
(404) 526-3641

Region 5
(Illinois, Indiana, Michigan, Minnesota, Ohio, Wisconsin)
300 W. Wacker Dr., Rm. 520
Chicago, IL 60606
(312) 353-1500

Region 6
(Arkansas, Louisiana, New Mexico, Oklahoma, Texas)
Federal Bldg., Rm. 13028
100 Commerce St.
Dallas, TX 75202

Region 7
(Iowa, Kansas, Missouri, Nebraska)
Old Federal Building
911 Walnut St.
Kansas City, MO 64106
(816) 374-5914

Region 8
(Colorado, Montana, North Dakota, South Dakota, Utah, Wyoming)
Lincoln Tower Bldg., Rm. 1140
1860 Lincoln St.
Denver, CO 80203
(303) 234-3271

Region 9
(American Samoa, Arizona, Guam, California, Trust Territory of the Pacific Islands, Hawaii, Nevada)
120 Montgomery St.
San Francisco, CA 94104
(415) 556-8794

Region 10
(Alaska, Idaho, Oregon, Washington)
1319 2nd Ave.
Arcade Bldg., Rm. M-16
Seattle, WA 98101
(206) 442-1486

FEDERAL DISASTER ASSISTANCE ADMINISTRATION

Department of Housing and Urban Development

★ REGIONAL OFFICES
● NATIONAL OFFICE

PUERTO RICO, VIRGIN ISLANDS	REGION 2
DISTRICT OF COLUMBIA	REGION 3
CANAL ZONE	REGION 4
AMERICAN SAMOA, GUAM	
TRUST TERRITORY OF THE	
PACIFIC ISLANDS	REGION 9

Map labels: BOSTON, NEW YORK, WASHINGTON D.C., PHILADELPHIA, ATLANTA, CHICAGO, KANSAS CITY, DALLAS, DENVER, SEATTLE, SAN FRANCISCO

Location of State Offices Responsible for Disaster Operations

State and FDAA Region	*Responsible Official*
Alabama 4	Director, Civil Defense Department State of Alabama 634 North Union Street Montgomery, AL 36104
Alaska 10	Director Alaska Disaster Office 1306 East 4th Avenue Anchorage, AK 99501
Arizona 9	Director State of Arizona Division of Emergency Services 5636 East McDowell Road Phoenix, AZ 85008
Arkansas 6	Director Office of Emergency Services P.O. Box 1144 Conway, AR 72032
California 9	Director Office of Emergency Services P.O. Box 9577 Sacramento, CA 95823
Colorado 8	Director of Disaster Emergency Services 300 Logan Street Denver, CO 80203
Connecticut 1	Director, Office of Civil Preparedness State of Connecticut Military Department State Armory, 360 Broad Street Hartford, CT 06115

Delaware 3	Director, Division of Emergency Planning and Operations Department of Public Safety Delaware City, DE 19706
District of Columbia 3	Director of Civil Defense District of Columbia Government Room 5007, Municipal Center 300 Indiana Avenue, N.W. Washington, DC 20001
Florida 4	Director Division of Disaster Preparedness Capital Office Plaza 1720 South Gadsden Street Tallahassee, FL 32301
Georgia 4	Director, State Civil Defense Department of Defense P.O. Box 18055 Atlanta, GA 30316
Hawaii 9	Director Office of Civil Defense Department of Defense State of Hawaii Fort Ruger, Building 24 Honolulu, HI 96816
Idaho 10	The Adjutant General of Idaho Military Division P.O. Box 45 Boise, ID 83707
Illinois 5	Director, Illinois Emergency Services and Disaster Agency 111 East Monroe Springfield, IL 62706
Indiana 5	Director Indiana Department of Civil Defense 100 North Senate Avenue Indianapolis, IN 46204

Iowa 7	Director Civil Defense Division B-33, Lucas State Office Building Des Moines, IA 50319
Kansas 7	State Disaster Programs Administrator State Office Building Topeka, KS 66612
Kentucky 4	Director of Disaster and Emergency Services Boone National Guard Center Frankfort, KY 40601
Louisiana 6	Director of Louisiana Civil Defense and Emergency Planning P.O. Box 44007, Capitol Station Baton Rouge, LA 70804
Maine 1	Director Bureau of Civil Emergency Preparedness State Office Building Augusta, ME 04330
Maryland 3	Director, Maryland Civil Defense and Emergency Planning Agency Pikesville, MD 21208
Massachusetts 1	Executive Secretary of Public Safety Massachusetts Civil Defense Agency and Office of Emergency Preparedness 905 Commonwealth Avenue Boston, MA 02215
Michigan 5	State Civil Defense Director Department of State Police 714 South Harrison Road East Lansing, MI 48824
Minnesota 5	Director, Minnesota Department of Public Safety B2-State Capitol St. Paul, MN 55155

Mississippi 4	Director Mississippi Civil Defense Council P.O. Box 4501, Fondren Station Jackson, MS 39216
Missouri 7	Coordinator Disaster Planning and Operations Office P.O. Box 116 Jefferson City, MO 65101
Montana 8	State Disaster Coordinator P.O. Box 1157 Helena, MT 59601
Nebraska 7	Director, Nebraska Civil Defense Agency National Guard Center 1300 Military Road Lincoln, NE 68508
Nevada 9	Director Nevada State Civil Defense and Disaster Agency 2525 South Carson Street Carson City, NV 87910
New Hampshire 1	Director, Office of Comprehensive State House Planning Concord, NH 03301
New Jersey 2	Director Civil Defense and Disaster Control Department of Defense P.O. Box 979 Eggerts Crossing Road Trenton, NJ 08625
New Mexico 6	State Planning Officer Legislative-Executive Building Santa Fe, NM 87501
New York 2	Chief of Staff to the Governor Division of Military and Naval Affairs Public Security Building State Campus Albany, NY 12226

North Carolina
4

State Coordinator
North Carolina Division of Civil
    Preparedness
Administration Building
116 West Jones Street
Raleigh, NC 27603

North Dakota
8

Director, Disaster Emergency Services
P.O. Box 1817
Bismarck, ND 58501

Ohio
5

Director of Disaster Services
State of Ohio
P.O. Box 660
Worthington, OH 43085

Oklahoma
6

Director
Oklahoma Civil Defense Agency
State Capitol Post Office Station
P.O. Box 53365
Oklahoma City, OK 73105

Oregon
10

Administrator
Division of Emergency Services
Oregon State Executive Department
8 Capitol Building
Salem, OR 97310

Pennsylvania
3

Director of Civil Defense
State Council of Civil Defense
Room B 151
Transportation and Safety Building
Harrisburg, PA 17120

Rhode Island
1

Director
Defense Civil Preparedness Agency
State House
Providence, RI 02903

South Carolina
4

Director
South Carolina Preparedness Agency
Rutledge Building
1429 Senate Street
Columbia, SC 29201

South Dakota 8	State Director of Civil Defense Camp Rapid Rapid City, SD 57701
Tennessee 4	Director, Division of Civil Defense and Emergency Preparedness National Guard Armory Sidco Drive Nashville, TN 37204
Texas 6	State Coordinator Defense and Disaster Safety P.O. Box 4087, North Austin Station Austin, TX 78773
Utah 8	Director, Utah State Office of Emergency Services State of Utah Council of Defense P.O. Box 8100 Salt Lake City, UT 84108
Vermont 1	Commissioner of Public Safety Civil Defense Division 132 State Street Montpelier, VT 05602
Virginia 3	State Coordinator of Emergency Services Office of the Governor 7700 Midlothian Turnpike Richmond, VA 23225
Washington 10	Director, Department of Emergency Services State of Washington 4220 East Martin Way Olympia, WA 98504
West Virginia 3	Director, Office of Emergency Services 806 Greenbrier Street Charleston, WV 25311

Wisconsin 5	Administrator Division of Emergency Government 4802 Sheboygan Avenue Madison, WI 53702
Wyoming 8	Coordinator Wyoming Disaster and Civil Defense Agency P.O. Box 1709 Cheyenne, WY 82001
American Samoa 9	Commissioner of Public Safety Government of American Samoa Office of the Governor Pago Pago, Tutuila American Samoa 96920
Canal Zone 4	Chief, Civil Defense Canal Zone Government Box M Balboa Heights, Canal Zone
Guam 9	Director, Bureau of Planning Territory of Guam P.O. Box 1651 Agana, GU 96910
Puerto Rico 2	Director Office of Civil Defense Commonwealth of Puerto Rico P.O. Box 5127, Puerta de Tierra Station San Juan, PR 00906
Trust Territory of the Pacific Islands 9	Disaster Control Officer Office of the High Commissioner Trust Territory of the Pacific Islands Saipan, Mariana Islands 96950
Virgin Islands 2	Director Office of Civil Defense Office of the Governor P.O. Box 296, Charlotte Amalie St. Thomas, VI 00801

Mortgage Insurance: Homes for Disaster Victims

FEDERAL AGENCY: Housing production and mortgage credit/FHA, Department of Housing and Urban Development.

OBJECTIVES: To help victims of a major disaster undertake homeownership on a sound basis.

TYPES OF ASSISTANCE: Guaranteed/Insured Loans.

USES AND USE RESTRICTIONS: HUD insures lenders against loss on mortgage loans. These loans may be used to finance the purchase of proposed, under construction, or existing single family housing for the occupant-mortgagor who is a victim of a major disaster. The maximum insurable loan for such an occupant mortgagor is $14,400. In order to qualify for assistance the home must be in an area designated by the President as a disaster area.

ELIGIBILITY REQUIREMENTS: *Applicant Eligibility:* Any family which is a victim of a major disaster as designated by the President is eligible to apply.

APPLICATION AND AWARD PROCESS: *Application Procedure:* Application is submitted for review and approval or disapproval to the local HUD Insuring or Area Office through an FHA-approved mortgage agency.

ASSISTANCE CONSIDERATION: *Formula and Matching Requirements:* The maximum amount of the loan is 100 percent of the FHA estimated value. No down payment is required. The current maximum interest rate is 7 percent plus one-half percent for mortgage insurance premium. The FHA application fee is $40 for existing, and $50 for proposed housing. The origination charge by the mortgagee varies, but may not normally exceed one percent of the total mortgage.

Length and Time Phasing of Assistance: The mortgage term may extend for 30 years, or three fourths of the property's remaining economic life, whichever is less, except 35 years if the mortgagor is unacceptable for a 30-year term and the property was constructed subject to FHA or VA inspection

INFORMATION CONTACTS: *Regional or Local Office:* Persons are encouraged to communicate with the nearest local HUD Area or Insuring Office. *Headquarters Office:* Director, Single Family Underwriting Division, Housing Production, and Mortgage Credit/FHA, Department of Housing and Urban Development, Washington, DC 20410. Telephone: (202) 755-5766.

Disaster Assistance

FEDERAL AGENCY: Federal Disaster Assistance Administration, Department of Housing and Urban Development.

OBJECTIVES: To provide assistance to states; local governments; owners of private, nonprofit medical care facilities; and individuals in alleviating suffering and hardship resulting from major disasters.

TYPES OF ASSISTANCE: Project Grants; Use of Property, Facilities and Equipment; Provision of Specialized Services.

USES AND USE RESTRICTIONS: Services are provided and grants and contributions are made available for pre-disaster assistance including suppression of forest or grass fires and for post-disaster assistance including repair or replacement of public facilities, and private, nonprofit medical care facilities; removal of wreckage and debris; performance of essential protective work on public and private lands; emergency shelter and temporary housing for displaced individuals and families; assistance to unemployed individuals; grants to local governments suffering loss of property tax revenue; emergency transportation service; and emergency communications.

ELIGIBILITY REQUIREMENTS: *Applicant Eligibility:* State and local governments in declared major disaster areas; owners of private, nonprofit medical care facilities; and individual disaster victims.

APPLICATION AND AWARD PROCESS: *Preapplication Coordination:* Governor makes a request for declaration of a major disaster by the President. Requests for assistance must be made by the governor in accordance with Part 2200.4, Title 24 of the Federal Disaster Assistance Regulations. Application Procedure: Upon declaration by the president that an area is a major disaster area, application for assistance is made through the State Coordinating Officer to the Federal Coordinating Officer appointed by FDAA.
Award Procedure: The Administrator of Federal Disaster Assistance allocates funds from the President's Disaster Relief Fund for use in a designated State Central Information Reception Agency and Department of the Treasury on SF 240. The Federal Coordinating Officer (usually the FDAA Director) then approves individual grants from his allocation on the basis of project applications filed by eligible applicants. Other Federal agencies are also reimbursed from this allocation for disaster work performed at FDAA's direction. States are responsible for distributing funds to local governments.

INFORMATION CONTACTS: *Regional or Local Offices:* HUD Regional Offices. Headquarters Office: Federal Disaster Assistance Administration, Department of Housing and Urban Development, Washington, DC 20410. Telephone: (202) 634-7820.

State Disaster Plans and Programs

FEDERAL AGENCY: Federal Disaster Assistance Administration, Department of Housing and Urban Development.

OBJECTIVES: To assist states in developing and maintaining comprehensive plans and practicable programs for preparation against major disasters including relief and assistance for individuals, business, and local governments following such disasters.

TYPES OF ASSISTANCE: Project Grants.

USES AND USE RESTRICTIONS: To improve disaster readiness and response capabilities.

ELIGIBILITY REQUIREMENTS: *Applicant Eligibility:* All states are eligible. Any state desiring assistance must designate or create an agency which is specially qualified to plan and administer a disaster relief program.

APPLICATION AND AWARD PROCESS: *Application Procedure:* State submits a letter to the appropriate FDAA Regional Office outlining its intent to create or designate an agency specially qualified to plan and administer such a disaster relief program.
Award Procedure: The Administrator, Federal Disaster Assistance, makes final decisions to approve state proposed plans. This office provides notification of grant

approval to the State Central Information Reception and Department of the Treasury on SF 240

INFORMATION CONTACTS: *Regional or Local Office:* Federal Disaster Assistance Administration Offices. *Headquarters Office:* Federal Disaster Assistance Administration, Department of Housing and Urban Development, Washington, DC 20410. Telephone: (202) 634-7820.

U.S. ARMY CORPS OF ENGINEERS
Civil Works Activities

Alabama
Mobile District
P.O. Box 2288
Mobile, AL 36628
(205) 473-0322, Ext. 411

Alaska
Alaska District
P.O. Box 7002
Anchorage, AK 99510
(907) 752-9114, 279-1132

Arkansas
Little Rock District
P.O. Box 867
Little Rock, AR 72203
(501) 372-4361, Ext. 5531

California
South Pacific Division
Rm. 1216
630 Sansome St.
San Francisco, CA 94111
(415) 556-0914

Los Angeles District
P.O. Box 2711
Los Angeles, CA 90053
(213) 688-5300

Sacramento District
650 Capitol Mall
Sacramento, CA 95814
(916) 449-2232

San Francisco District
100 McAllister St.
San Francisco, CA 94102
(415) 556-3660

Florida
Jacksonville District
P.O. Box 4970
Jacksonville, FL 32201
(904) 791-2241

Georgia
South Atlantic Division
510 Title Bldg.,
30 Pryor St., S.W.
Atlanta, GA 30303
(404) 526-6711

Savannah District,
P.O. Box 889
Savannah, GA 31402
(912) 233-8822, Ext. 226

Hawaii
Pacific Ocean Division
Bldg. 96
Ft. Armstrong,
Honolulu, HI 96813
(808) 543-2615

Illinois
North Central Division
536 S. Clark St.
Chicago, IL 60605
(312) 353-6310

Chicago District
219 S. Dearborn St.
Chicago, IL 60604
(312) 353-6400

Rock Island District,
Clock Tower Bldg.
Rock Island, IL 61201
(309) 788-6361, Ext. 224

Kentucky
Louisville District
P.O. Box 59
Louisville, KY 40201
(502) 582-5601

Louisiana
New Orleans District
P.O. Box 60267
New Orleans, LA 70160
(504) 582-5601

Maryland
Baltimore District
P.O. Box 1715
Baltimore, MD 21203
(301) 962-4545

Massachusetts
New England Division
424 Trapelo Rd.
Waltham, MA 02154
(617) 894-2400, Ext. 220

Michigan
Detroit District
P.O. Box 1027
Detroit, MI 48231
(313) 226-6762

Minnesota
St. Paul District
1210 USPO & Custom House
St. Paul, MN 55101
(612) 725-7501

Mississippi
Lower Mississippi Valley Division
P.O. Box 80
Vicksburg, MS 39180
(601) 636-1311, Ext. 201

Vicksburg District
P.O. Box 60
Vicksburg, MS 39180
(601) 636-1311, Ext. 401

Missouri
Kansas City District
700 Federal Bldg.
601 East 12th St.
Kansas City, MO 64106
(806) 374-3201

St. Louis District
210 N. 12th St.
St. Louis, MO 63101
(314) 268-2821

Nebraska
Missouri River Division
P.O. Box 103
Downtown Station
Omaha, NE 63101
(402) 221-3001

Omaha District
7410 USPO & Courthouse
215 N. 17th St.
Omaha, NE 68102
(402) 221-3900

New Mexico
Albuquerque District
P.O. Box 1580
Albuquerque, NM 87103
(505) 843-2732

New York
North Atlantic Division
90 Church St.
New York, NY 10007
(212) 264-7101

Buffalo District
1776 Niagara St.
Buffalo, NY 14207

New York District
26 Federal Plaza
New York, NY 10007
(212) 264-0100

New York Harbor, Supervisor of
26 Federal Plaza
New York, NY 10007
(212) 264-0100

North Carolina
Wilmington District
P.O. Box 1890
Wilmington, NC 28401
(919) 763-9971

Oklahoma
Tulsa District,
P.O. Box 61
Tulsa, OK 74102
(918) 584-7151, Ext. 7311

Oregon
North Pacific Division
Custom House, Rm. 210
Portland, OR 97209
(503) 226-3361, Ext. 2500

Portland District
P.O. Box 2946
Portland, OR 97208
(503) 777-4441, Ext. 200

Pennsylvania
Philadelphia District
U.S. Custom House
2nd & Chestnut Sts.
Philadelphia, PA 19106
(215) 597-4849

Pittsburgh District
Federal Bldg.
1000 Liberty Ave.
Pittsburgh, PA 15222
(412) 644-6800

South Carolina
Charleston District
P.O. Box 919
Charleston, SC 29402
(803) 577-4171, Ext. 229

Tennessee
Memphis District
668 Federal Office Bldg.
Memphis, TN 38103
(901) 534-3221

Nashville District
P.O. Box 1070
Nashville, TN 37202
(615) 749-5626

Texas
Southwestern Division
1114 Commerce St.
Dallas, TX 75202
(214) 749-3336

Fort Worth District
P.O. Box 17300
Fort Worth, TX 76102
(817) 334-2300

Galveston District
P.O. Box 1229
Galveston, TX 77550
(713) 763-1211, Ext. 301

Virginia
Norfolk District
803 Front St.
Norfolk, VA 23510
(703) 625-8201, Ext 231

Washington
 Seattle District
 1519 Alaskan Way South
 Seattle, WA 98134
 (206) 682-2700

 Walla Walla District
 Bldg. 602
 City-County Airport
 Walla Walla, WA 99362
 (509) 525-5500, Ext. 100

West Virginia
 Huntington District
 P.O. Box 2127
 Huntington, WV 25721
 (304) 529-2318, Ext. 253

Flood Control Works and Federally Authorized Coastal Protection Works, Rehabilitation

FEDERAL AGENCY: Office of the Chief of Engineers, Department of the Army, Department of Defense.

OBJECTIVES: To assist in the repair and restoration of flood of control works damaged by flood or federally authorized hurricane-flood and shore protection works damaged by extraordinary wind, wave, or water action.

TYPES OF ASSISTANCE: Provision of Specialized Services.

USES AND USE RESTRICTIONS: Authorized assistance includes emergency repair or rehabilitation of flood control works damaged by flood and restoration of federally authorized coastal protection structures damaged by extraordinary wind, wave, or water action. Assistance does not extend to major improvements or betterments of flood control of federally authorized coastal protection structures, nor to reimbursement of individuals or communities for funds expended in repair or rehabilitation efforts. Local interests are normally required to (a) provide without cost to the United States all lands, easements, and rights-of-ways necessary for the authorized work; (b) hold and save the United States free from damages due to the authorized work; (c) maintain and operate, in a manner satisfactory to the Chief of Engineers, all the protective works after completion of repairs. Additionally, work constituting deferred regular maintenance and desired major modifications may be included at local cost.

ELIGIBILITY REQUIREMENTS: *Applicant Eligibility:* Owners of damaged protective works or state and local officials of public entities responsible for their maintenance, repair, and operation.

APPLICATION AND AWARD PROCESS: *Application Procedure:* Written application by letter or by form request if such a form is locally used by the District Engineer of the Corps of Engineers.
Award Procedure: Formal notice of approval and/or disapproval will be furnished applicant by the District Engineer of the Corps of Engineers.

INFORMATION CONTACTS: *Regional or Local Office:* U.S. Army Division or District Engineers. *Headquarters Office:* Director of Civil Works, Office of the Chief of Engineers, Department of the Army, Washington, DC 20314. Telephone (202) 693-6875.

Flood Fighting and Rescue Operations, and Emergency Protection of Coastal Protective Works Federally Authorized

FEDERAL AGENCY: Office of the Chief of Engineers, Department of the Army, Department of Defense.

OBJECTIVES: To provide emergency assistance as required to supplement local efforts and capabilities in time of flood or coastal storm.

TYPES OF ASSISTANCE: Provision of Specialized Services.

USES AND USE RESTRICTIONS: Emergency assistance in all phases of flood fighting and rescue operations is provided to supplement local efforts. State and local governments must use their own resources to maximum extent feasible, usually including the furnishing of common labor. No specific restrictions are placed upon such assistance.

ELIGIBILITY REQUIREMENTS: *Applicant Eligibilty:* State or local public agencies.

APPLICATION AND AWARD PROCESS: *Applicant Procedure.* Oral or written request by responsible state or local agencies.

INFORMATION CONTACTS: *Regional or Local Office:* U.S. Army Division or District Engineers. *Headquarters Office:* Director of Civil Works, Office of the Chief of Engineers, Department of the Army, Washington, DC 20314. Telephone: (202) 693-6875.

Flood Plain Management Services

FEDERAL AGENCY: Office of the Chief of Engineers, Department of the Army, Department of Defense.

OBJECTIVES: To promote appropriate recognition of flood hazards in land and water use planning and development through the provision of needed information, technical services, and guidance.

TYPES OF ASSISTANCE: Dissemination of Technical Information; Advisory Services and Counseling.

USES AND USE RESTRICTIONS: Available information identifies areas subject to flooding and flood losses from streams, lakes, and oceans and describes flood hazard at proposed building sites. It can be used as a basis for planning flood plain use, for delineating boundaries for flood plain regulations, for setting elevations for flood proofing, and for indicating areas to be acquired for open space. Activities also include interpretation of technical information and related planning assistance and guidance toward wise use of flood plains. Services are available within annual funding limitations from district offices on request. The only exception is that services to individuals are limited to available information. It is intended that information be used in planning and its availability publicized.

ELIGIBILITY REQUIREMENTS: *Applicant Eligibility:* States, political subdivisions of states, other public organizations, and individuals as indicated under Restrictions.

APPLICATION AND AWARD PROCESS: *Preapplication Coordination:* Although not required, discussion of problem and needs with district engineer's Flood Plain

Management Service representative would facilitate request.

Application Procedure: Requests are made in the form of a letter to the district engineer documenting the need for assistance. The formal flood plain information report is coordinated through a designated state agency and requires some assurances.

Award Procedure: After approval by division engineer, request takes its place among others and is responded to as capability permits, however, response time and approval time may be the same for information readily available. Services and information are provided directly to the applicant except for flood plain information reports which are coodinated through the designated state agency.

INFORMATION CONTACTS: Regional or Local Office: Persons are encouraged to communicate with the district engineer of the nearest U.S. Army District; Attn: FPMS. *Headquarters Office:* Director of Civil Works, Attn. FPMS Office, Chief of Engineers, Department of the Army, Washington, DC 20314. Telephone: (202) 693-1691.

CIVIL DEFENSE PREPAREDNESS AGENCY
Field Offices

REGION 1

(New Jersey, New York)
Regional Director
26 Federal Plaza, Rm. 2354
New York, NY 10007
(201) 264-9856

REGION 6

(Iowa, Kans., Missouri, Neb.)
Regional Director
Traders National Bank, Bldg.,
    Rm. 1510
1125 Grand Ave.
Kansas City, MO 64106

Regional Offices

California

(Region 7: American Samoa,
California, Arizona, Hawaii,
Nevada, Guam)
P.O. Box 7287
Santa Rosa, CA 95401
(707) 544-1330

Colorado

(Region 6: Colorado, Iowa,
Kansas, Missouri, Nebraska,
North Dakota, South Dakota,
Utah, Wyoming)
Denver Federal Building, #710
Denver, CO 80225
(303) 234-2553

Georgia

(Region 3: Alabama, Florida,
Georgia, Mississippi, North
Carolina, South Carolina,
Tenn, Canal Zone, Kentucky)
Thomasville, GA 31792
(912) 226-1761

Maryland

(Region 2: Delaware, District of
Columbia, Maryland, Pa.,
Virginia, W. Virginia)
Olney, MD 20832

Massachusetts

(Region 1: Conn., Maine,
Mass., New Hampshire, New
Jersey, New York, Puerto
Rico, Rhode Island, Vermont,
Virgin Islands)
Federal Regional Center
Manyard, MA 01754
(617) 897-9381

Michigan

(Region 4: Illinois, Ohio,
Ind., Mich., Minn., Wisc.)
Federal Center
Battle Creek, MI 49016
(606) 986-8142

Texas

(Region 5; Arkansas, N.M.,
Louisiana, Okla., Tex.)
Federal Regional Center
Denton, TX 76201
(817) 387-5811

Washington

(Region 8: Alaska, Idaho,
Montana, Oregon, Wash.)
Federal Regional Center
Bothell, WA 98011
(206) 486-0721

Civil Defense Emergency Water Supply Equipment

FEDERAL AGENCY: Defense Civil Preparedness Agency, Department of Defense.

OBJECTIVES: To restore temporarily water supplies in communities suffering shortages from enemy attack. Also used to assist states and communities in overcoming severe water shortages and natural disaster emergencies.

TYPES OF ASSISTANCE: Use of Property, Facilities, and Equipment.

USES AND USE RESTRICTIONS: Equipment consisting of electric generators, pipes, couplings, pumps, purifers, chlorinators, and storage tanks for use by communities to pump water from lakes or streams to local reservoirs in areas where normal water supplies have failed and to pump water from basements of public buildings, hospitals, and other flooded areas after experiencing tornadoes, floods, and hurricanes. Loans are usually on 90-day basis but may be extended if conditions warrant. The government loans directly to the state. Ownership remains in the government, with the state receiving temporary possession only. Community is responsible for cost of transportation from and return of property to federal storage.

ELIGIBILITY REQUIREMENTS: *Applicant Eligibility:* State and through the state their instrumentalities, and local (city, county, township, etc.) governments.

APPLICATION AND AWARD PROCESS: *Application Procedure:* All local applications must be sent to the state civil defense agency. Direct request at time of need by rapid communication.

INFORMATION CONTACTS: *Regional or Local Office:* DCPA Regional Offices. Applicant governments are encouraged to communicate with the state civil defense director through their local civil defense director. *Headquarters Office:* Assistance Director for Plans and Operations, Defense Civil Preparedness Agency, Washington, DC 20301. Telephone: (202) 697-2186

U.S. DEPARTMENT OF AGRICULTURE
Farmers Home Administration State Offices

Alabama
Aronov Bldg, Rm 717
474 S. Court St.
Montgomery, AL 36104
(205) 265-5611, Ext. 302

Arizona
Federal Bldg., Rm. 6081
230 N. First Ave.
Phoenix, AZ 85025
(602) 261-3191

Arkansas
P.O. Box 2778
Little Rock, AR 72203
(501) 378-5436

California
(Nevada, Hawaii)
459 Cleveland St.
Woodland, CA 95695
(916) 449-3308

Colorado
New Federal Bldg., Rm. 231
No. 1 Diamond Plaza
2490 West 26th Ave.
Denver, CO 80211
(303) 837-4347

Georgia
Peachtree 25th Bldg., Suite 900
1720 Peachtree St., N.W.
Atlanta, GA 30309
(404) 526-3924

Idaho
Federal Bldg., Rm. 402
304 N. Eighth St.
Boise, ID 83702
(208) 342-2711

Illinois
2106 W. Springfield Ave.
Champaign, IL 61820
(217) 356-1127

Indiana
Suite 1700
5610 Crawfordsville Rd.
Indianapolis, IN 46224
(317) 633-8481

Iowa
Federal Bldg., Rm. 873
210 Walnut St.
Des Moines, IA 40309
(515) 284-4121

Kansas
New England Bldg., Rm. 630
Fifth and Kansas
Topeka, KS 66603
(913) 234-8661

Kentucky
333 Waller Ave.
Lexington, KY 40504
(606) 252-2312, Ext. 2733

Louisiana
3723 Government St.
Alexandria, LA 71301
(318) 443-7391

Maine
USDA Office Bldg.
Orono, ME 04473
(207) 866-4929

Michigan
1405 S. Harrison Rd.
East Lansing, MI 48823
(517) 372-1910, Ext. 272

Minnesota
U.S. Courthouse
252 Federal Office Bldg.
St. Paul, MN 55101
(612) 725-7695

Mississippi
Milner Bldg., Rm. 528
Jackson, MS 39201
(601) 948-7821, Ext. 372

Missouri
Parkade Plaza
Terrace Level,
Columbia, MO 65201
(314) 442-2271, Ext. 3168

Montana
P.O. Box 850
Bozeman, MT 59715
(406) 587-4511

Nebraska
Federal Bldg. & Courthouse,
    Rm. 430
129 North 10th St.
Lincoln, NE 68508
(402) 475-3342

New Jersey
(Delaware, D.C., Maryland)
P.O. Box 1222
Newark, DE 19711
(302) 731-8310

New Mexico
Federal Bldg., Rm. 3414
517 Gold Ave. S.W.
Albuquerque, NM 87101
(505) 843-0311, Ext. 2462

New York
Midtown Plaza, Rm. 203
700 East Water St.
Syracuse, NY 13210
(315) 473-3458

North Carolina
Federal Bldg., Rm. 514
310 New Bern Ave.
Raleigh, NC 27611
(919) 755-4640

North Dakota
P.O. Box 1737
Bismarck, ND 58501
(701) 225-4011, Ext. 4237

Ohio
Old Post Office Bldg., Rm. 316
Columbus, OH 43215
(614) 469-5606

Oklahoma
Agricultural Center Office Bldg.
Farm Rd.
Stillwater, OK 74074
(405) 372-7111, Ext. 239

Oregon (Alaska)
1218 S.W. Washington St.
Portland, OR 97205
(503) 221-2731

Pennsylvania
Federal Bldg.
228 Walnut St.
P.O. Box 905
Harrisburg, PA 17108
(717) 782-4476

Puerto Rico
(Virgin Islands)
GPO Box 6106G
San Juan, PR 00936
722-3508

South Carolina
Federal Office Bldg.
901 Sumter St.
Columbia, SC 29201
(803) 765-5876

South Dakota
P.O. Box 821
Huron, SD 57350
(605) 352-8651, Ext.311

Tennessee
538 U.S. Court House Bldg.,
801 Broadway
Nashville, TN 37203
(615) 749-5501

Texas
3910 South General Bruce Dr.
Temple, TX 76501
(817) 773-1711

Utah
Federal Bldg., Rm. 5311
125 South State St.
Salt Lake City, UT 84138

Vermont
(Connecticut, Massachusetts,
New Hampshire,
Rhode Island)
P.O. Box 588
Montpelier, VT 05602
(802) 223-2371

Virginia
P.O. Box 10106
Richmond, VA 23240
(804) 782-2451

Washington
127 S. Mission St.
Wenatchee, WA 98801
(509) 662-5161

West Virginia
P.O. Box 678
Morgantown, WV 26505
(304) 599-7791

Wisconsin
P.O. Box 639
Stevens Point, WI 54481
(715) 341-5900

Wyoming
P.O. Box 820
Casper, WY 82601

To locate County Farmers Home Administration Offices, consult your telephone directory under U.S. Department of Agriculture, or the State Office of the Farmers Home Administration listed above.

Emergency Loans

FEDERAL AGENCY: Farmers Home Administration, Department of Agriculture.

OBJECTIVES: To assist farmers, ranchers, and oyster planters to cover losses resulting from designated disasters so that they may continue farming or livestock operations with credit from other sources, including FmHA Farm Operating and Farm ownership loans.

TYPES OF ASSISTANCE: Guaranteed/Insurance Loans.

USES AND USE RESTRICTIONS: (a) Replacement equipment and livestock damaged or destroyed by natural disasters, (b) make real estate repairs made necessary by natural disasters, and (c) under certain conditions refinance secured and unsecured debts made necessary by the disaster. These loans are not made to finance new farming, ranching, or oyster planting operations. Instead, the loan is made to cover expenses that went into damaged or destroyed crops up to the time of the disaster. The total amount of loan for all purposes must not exceed the dollar losses sustained and has to be within the applicant's repayment ability and must meet FmHA secruity requirements. For losses of a physical nature, emergency loans will be based on the cost of repairing, replacing, and restoring damaged farm property, including essential home furnishings and personal possessions. Applicants may be reimbursed for expenses already incurred for such purposes. Loans that are based on qualifying production losses may include funds to repay applicants for production expenses which went into their damaged or destroyed crop and livestock enterprises. In all cases, applicants will be required to furnish itemized statements of expenditures for which they are requesting reimbursement. These loans are made in counties (1) named by the Federal Disaster Assistance Administration as eligible for Federal Assistance under a presidential declaration of a major disaster and (2) designated as emergency loan areas by the Secretary of Agriculture and (3) authorized by the FHA State Director where he finds that not more than 25 farmers or ranchers in a county have been affected by the disaster.

ELIGIBILITY REQUIREMENTS: *Applicant Eligibility:* (a) Established farmer or rancher (either tenant or owner-operated), (b) citizen of United States, (c) severe crop losses or property damage caused by a natural disaster, not compensated for by insurance or otherwise, (d) good character and with necessary ability to succeed, (e) manages his farming or ranching operations. Applicants who cannot meet these requirements are not eligible.

APPLICATION AND AWARD PROCESS: *Application Procedure:* Application form provided by the Farmers Home Administration must be presented to the FHA county office servicing the applicant's county. FmHA personnel assist applicants in completing application form.

Award Procedure: FmHA County Supervisors. District Directors, and State Directors are authorized to approve these loans, subject to certain administrative requirements, after applicants are determined eligible by County or Area Committees.

INFORMATION CONTACTS: *Regional or Local Office:* Consult your local telephone directory for FmHA county office number. If no listing, get in touch with appropriate FmHA state office.

Headquarters Office: Administrator, Farmers Home Administration, U.S. Department of Agriculture, Washington, DC. Telephone: (202) 447-7967.

Emergency Conservation Measures

FEDERAL AGENCY: Agricultural Stabilization and Conservation Service, Department of Agriculture.

OBJECTIVES: To enable farmers to perform emergency conservation measures to control wind erosion on farmlands, or to rehabilitate farmlands damaged by wind erosion, floods, hurricanes, or other natural disasters.

TYPES OF ASSISTANCE: Project Grants.

USES AND USE RESTRICTIONS: Emergency cost-sharing is limited to new conservation problems in secretarially or presidentially declared disaster areas created by natural disasters which: if not treated will impair or endanger the land; materially affect the productive capacity of the land; represent damage which is unusual in character and, except for wind erosion, is not the type which, would recur frequently in the same area; and will be so costly to rehabilitate that federal assistance is or will be required to return the land to productive agricultural use.

ELIGIBILITY REQUIREMENTS: *Applicant Eligibility:* Any person who as owner, landlord, tenant, or sharecropper on a farm or ranch, including associated groups, bears a part of the cost of an approved conservation practice in a secretarially or presidentially declared disaster area is eligible to apply for cost-share conservation assistance.

APPLICATION AND AWARD PROCESS: *Application Procedure:* Eligible persons make application on Form ASCS-245, for cost-sharing at any time during the year, at the Agricultural Stabilization and Conservation Service (ASCS) county office for the county in which the land is located.

Award Procedure: The Agricultural Stabilization and Conservation (ASC) county committee must approve applications in whole or in part within the county allocation of federal funds for that purpose.

INFORMATION CONTACTS: *Regional or Local Office:* Farmers are advised to contact their local county Agricultural Stabilization and Conservation Service office after a natural disaster has occurred to determine whether the county has been designated eligible for emergency cost-share assistance. Consult the local telephone directory for location of the ASCS county office. *Headquarters Office:* Agricultural Stabilization and Conservation Service, U.S. Department of Agriculture, Washington, DC 20250.

SMALL BUSINESS ADMINISTRATION
Regional and District Offices

REGION 1
(Connecticut, Maine,
New Hampshire,
Massachusetts, Rhode Island,
and Vermont)
  Regional Director
  John F. Kennedy Federal Bldg.
  Rm. 2113
  Boston, MA 02203
  (617) 223-2100

District Offices:
  1326 Appleton St.
  Holyoke, MA 01040
  (413) 536-8770

  Federal Bldg.
  40 Western Ave., Rm. 512
  Augusta, ME 04330
  (207) 622-6171

  55 Pleasant St., Rm. 213
  Concord, NH 03301
  (603) 224-4041

  Federal Bldg.
  450 Main St., Rm. 710
  Hartford, CT 06103
  (203) 244-2000

  Federal Bldg.
  87 State St., Rm. 210
  Montpelier, VT 05602
  (802) 223-7472

  57 Eddy St., Rm. 710
  Providence, RI 02903
  (401) 528-1000

REGION 2
(New Jersey, New York,
Puerto Rico, Virgin Islands)
  Regional Director
  26 Federal Plaza, Rm. 3930
  New York, NY 10007
  (212) 460-0100

District Offices:
  225 Ponce de Leon Ave.
  Hato Rey, PR 00919
  (809) 765-0404

  970 Broad St., Rm. 1635
  Newark, NJ 07102
  (201) 645-3000

  Hunter Plaza
  Fayette & Salina Sts., Rm. 308
  Syracuse, NY 13202
  (315) 473-3350

  Chamber of Commerce Bldg.
  55 St. Paul St.
  Rochester, NY 14604
  (716) 546-4900

REGION 3
(Delaware, District of Columbia,
Maryland, Pennsylvania, Virginia,
West Virginia)
  Regional Director
  1 Decker Square
  East Lobby, Suite 400
  Bala Cynwyd, PA 19004
  (215) 597-3311

District Offices:
109 North 3rd St., Rm. 301
Lowndes Bldg.
Clarksburg, WV 26301
(304) 624-3461

Federal Bldg.
1000 Liberty Ave., Rm. 1401
Pittsburgh, PA 15222
(412) 644-3311

Federal Bldg.
400 North 8th St., Rm. 3015
Richmond, VA 23240
(703) 782-2000

REGION 4
(Alabama, Florida, Georgia,
Kentucky, Mississippi, North
Carolina, South Carolina,
Tennessee)
Regional Director
1401 Peachtree St., NE, Rm. 441
Atlanta, GA 30309

District Offices:
908 South 20th St., Rm. 202
Birmingham, AL 35205
(205) 325-3011

222 S. Church St., Rm. 500
Addison Bldg.
Charlotte, NC 28202
(704) 372-0711

1801 Assembly St., Rm. 117
Columbia, SC 29201
(803) 765-5376

Petroleum Bldg., Suite 690
Pascagoula & Amite Sts.
Jackson, MS 39205
(601) 948-7821

Federal Bldg.
400 West Bay St., Rm. 261
Jacksonville, FL 32202
(904) 791-2011

Federal Bldg.
600 Federal Pl., Rm. 188
Louisville, KY 40202
(502) 582-5011

Federal Bldg.
51 Southwest 1st Ave., Rm. 912
Miami, FL 33130
(305) 350-5011

500 Union St., Rm. 301
Nashville, TN 37219
(615) 749-9300

502 S. Gay St., Rm. 307
Fidelity Bankers Bldg.
Knoxville, TN 37902
(615) 524-4011

REGION 5
(Illinois, Indiana, Michigan, Min-
nesota, Ohio, Wisconsin)
Regional Director
Federal Bldg.
219 S. Dearborn St., Rm. 437
Chicago, IL 60604
(312) 353-4400

District Offices:
502 E. Monroe St.
Ridgely Bldg., Rm. 816
Springfield, IL 62701
(217) 525-4200

1240 East 9th St., Rm. 5524
Cleveland, OH 44199
(216) 522-3131

34 North High St.
Columbus, OH 43215
(614) 469-6600

Federal Bldg.
550 Main St.
Cincinnati, OH 45202
(513) 684-2200

1249 Washington Blvd., Rm.1200
Book Bldg.
Detroit, MI 48226
(313) 226-6000

36 S. Pennsylvania St., Rm. 108
Century Bldg.
Indianapolis, IN 46204
(317) 633-7000

122 W.Washington Ave.,Rm.713
Madison, WI 53703
(608) 256-4441

12 S. 6th St.
Plymouth Bldg.
Minneapolis, MN 55402
(612) 725-4242

REGION 6
(Arkansas, Louisiana, New Mexico,
Oklahoma, Texas)
  Regional Director
  1100 Commerce St., Rm. 300
  Dallas, TX 75202
  (214) 749-5611

District Offices:
  Federal Bldg. & Courthouse
  500 Goald Ave., S.W.
  Albuquerque, NM 87101
  (505) 843-0311

808 Travis St., Rm. 1219
Niels Esperson Bldg.
Houston, TX 77002
(713) 226-4011

Post Office & Court House Bldg.
West Capital Ave., Rm. 377
Little Rock, AR 72201
(501) 378-5871

1205 Texas Ave.
Lubbock, TX 79408
(806) 747-3711

219 East Jackson St.
Harlingen, TX 78550
(Lower Rio Grande Valley)
(512) 423-8933

505 East Travis St., Rm. 201
Travis Terrace Bldg.
Marshall, TX 75670
(214) 935-4257

Plaza Tower, 17th Floor
1001 Howard Ave.
New Orleans, LA 70113
(504) 527-2611

30 North Hudson St., Rm. 501
Mercantile Bldg.
Oklahoma City, OK 73102
(405) 231-4011

301 Broadway, Rm. 300
Manion Bldg.
San Antonio, TX 78205
(512) 225-5511

REGION 7
(Iowa, Kansas, Missouri,
Nebraska)
  Regional Director
  Walnut St., 24th Floor
  Kansas City, MO 64106
  (816) 374-7000

District Offices:
  New Federal Bldg.
  210 Walnut St., Rm. 749
  Des Moines, IA 50309
  (515) 284-4000

  Federal Bldg.
  215 N. 17th St., Rm. 7419
  Omaha, NE 68102
  (402) 221-1221

  Federal Bldg.
  210 N. 12th St., Rm. 520
  St. Louis, MO 63101
  (314) 622-8100

  120 S. Market St., Rm. 301
  Wichita, KS 67202
  (316) 267-6311

REGION 8
(Colorado, Montana,
North Dakota,
South Dakota, Utah, Wyoming)
  Regional Director
  721 19th St., Rm. 426A
  Denver, CO 80202

District Offices:
  Federal Bldg., Rm. 4001
  100 East B St.
  Casper, WY 82601
  (307) 265-5550

  Federal Bldg.
  653 2nd Ave., North, Rm. 218
  Fargo, ND 58102
  (701) 237-5771

  Power Block Bldg.
  Corner Main & 6th Ave., Rm. 208
  Helena, MT 442-9040

  Federal Bldg.
  125 S. State St., Rm. 2237
  Salt Lake City, UT 84111
  (801) 524-5500

  National Bank Bldg.
  8th & Main Ave., Rm. 402
  Sioux Falls, SD 57102
  (605) 336-2980

REGION 9
(Arizona, California, Hawaii,
Nevada, Pacific Islands)
  Regional Director
  Federal Bldg.
  450 Golden Gate Ave.
  San Francisco, CA 94102
  (415) 556-9000

District Offices:
  149 Bethel St., Rm. 402
  Honolulu, HI 96813
  (808) 546-8950

  849 S. Broadway
  Los Angeles, CA 90014
  (213) 688-2121

  112 N. Central Ave.
  Phoenix, AZ 85004
  (602) 261-3900

110 West C St.
San Diego, CA 92101
(714) 293-5000

REGION 10
(Alaska, Idaho, Oregon,
Washington)
Regional Director
710 2nd Ave.
Dexter Horton Bldg., 5th Floor
Seattle, WA 98104
(206) 442-0111

District Offices:
1016 W. 6th Ave., Suite 200
Anchorage Legal Center
Anchorage, AK 99501
(907) 272-5561

503 3rd Ave.
Fairbanks, AK 99701
(907) 452-5561

216 N. 9th St., Rm. 408
Boise, ID 83701
(208) 342-2711

921 Southwest Washington St.
Portland, OR 97205
(503) 221-2000

Court House Bldg., Rm. 651
Spokane, WA 99210
(509) 456-0111

Displaced Business Loans

FEDERAL AGENCY: Small Business Administration.

OBJECTIVES: To assist small businesses to continue in business, purchase a business, or establish a new business if substantial economic injury has been suffered as a result of displacement by, or location in or near, a federally aided project.

TYPES OF ASSISTANCE: Direct Loans; Guaranteed/Insured Loans.

USES AND USE RESTRICTIONS: Excludes speculation, nonprofit seeking enterprise, selling business to strangers, paying off principals or unsecured creditors, holding real property primarily for sale or investment, agricultural activity, and monopoly. Personal and business assets and other means of credit at reasonable terms must be utilized where feasible. No maximum loan amount, maturity and maximum is 30 years; the interest rate-bank share of loan legal and reasonable set quarterly; SBA share established by legislative formula annually.

ELIGIBILITY REQUIREMENTS: *Applicant Eligibility:* Most small businesses, which suffer physical displacement and/or economic injury as a result of a federally aided urban renewal, highway, or other construction project.

APPLICATION AND AWARD PROCESS: *Application Procedure:* Applications are filed in the field office serving that territory, provided there is mutual agreement between the two field offices involved.
Award Procedure: Applicant is notified of approval by authorization letter from district SBA offices.

INFORMATION CONTACTS: *Regional or Local Office:* Field offices (regional and district). *Headquarters Office:* Director, Office of Financing, Small Business Administration, 1441 L St., N.W., Washington, DC 20416. Telephone: (202) 382-4987.

Economic Injury Disaster Loans

FEDERAL AGENCY: Small Business Administration

OBJECTIVES: To assist business concerns suffering economic injury as a result of certain presidential, SBA, and Department of Agriculture disaster designations.

TYPES OF ASSISTANCE: Direct Loans.

USES AND USE RESTRICTIONS: Currently 5 percent for up to 30 years for repayment in amounts up to $500,000 SBA share, to any one small concern or group of affiliated concerns. Funds can be provided to pay current liabilities which the small concern could have paid if the disaster had not occurred. Working capital for a limited period can be provided to continue the business in operations until conditions return to normal. No funds available for realty, equipment repair, or acquisition; the interest rate may vary according to date or disaster and governing disaster legislation. A direct loan or SBA share of an immediate participation loan is limited to $500,000. Additional amounts are available as guaranteed loans made by a financial institution.

ELIGIBILITY REQUIREMENTS: *Applicant Eligibility:* Must be a small business concern as described in SBA rules and regulations. Must furnish evidence of the extent of economic injury claimed.

APPLICATION AND AWARD PROCESS: *Preapplication Coordination:* Generally preapplication interviews are held to acquaint applicant with general approach to establishing eligibility and what assistance may be available.
Application Procedure: Applications are filed with nearest SBA on-field office on one copy of SF 5 provided for this purpose.
Award Procedure: Applicant is notified of approval by authorization letter from district SBA office.

INFORMATION CONTACTS: *Regional or Local Office:* Field Offices (regional, district, and branch). *Headquarters Office:* Office of Disaster Operations, Small Business Administration, 1441 L St., N.W., Washington DC 20416.
Telephone (202) 382-3175.

Physical Disaster Loans

FEDERAL AGENCY: Small Business Administration.

OBJECTIVE: To provide loans to restore, as nearly as possible, the victims of physical type disaster to predisaster condition.

TYPES OF ASSISTANCE: Direct Loans.

USES AND USE RESTRICTIONS: Loans at 5 percent interest rate for anyone without regard to ability to provide needed funds from private sources. (Interest rates may vary depending on date disaster occurred and governing legislation.) Loans are made for up to 30 years. Loan funds may be used to repair or replace damaged or destroyed realty, machinery, and equipment, household and other personal property. Funds must be used for the purposes stipulated in an authorization which is issued in connection with each approved plan. Loans are not available to those engaged in agriculture, and no part of a loan to an otherwise eligible borrower can be used for agricultural purposes.

ELIGIBILITY REQUIREMENTS: *Applicant Eligibility:* Must have suffered physical property loss as a result of a disaster which occurred in an area designated as eligible for assistance by the Administration as a result of floods, riots, or civil disturbances, or other catastrophes. Individuals, business concerns, churches, private schools, colleges and universities, and hospitals are eligible to apply for assistance.

APPLICATION AND AWARD PROCESS: *Preapplication Coordination:* Whenever feasible, interviews are held with disaster victims and the program is explained.

Assistance on filing of application is provided.
Award Procedure: Applicant is notified of approval by authorization letter from disaster or district SBA office.

INFORMATION CONTACTS: *Regional or Local Office:* Field Offices (area, region, and district). *Headquarters Office:* Office of Disaster Operations, Small Business Administration, 1441 L St., N.W., Washington, DC 20416. Telephone: (202) 382-3175.

Product Disaster Loans

FEDERAL AGENCY: Small Business Administration.

OBJECTIVES: To assist small business concerns which have suffered economic injury as a result of inability to market a product for human consumption because of a finding of toxicity in the product.

TYPES OF ASSISTANCE: Direct Loans.

USES AND USE RESTRICTIONS: Currently 5 percent loans up to 30 years for repayment in amounts of up to $500,000; SBA share to any one small concern or group of affiliated concerns for a business loan. Funds can be used to pay current liabilities the small concern could otherwise have paid if the disaster had not occurred. Funds also available for working capital purposes and to certain limited extents to acquire equipment or facilities necessary to meet health or sanitary requirements to make a marketable product. Funds are restricted to the loss proven to be caused by the specific finding which created inability to market a product intended for human consumption. A direct loan or SBA share of an immediate participation loan is limited to $500,000 to any one small concern or affiliated group of concerns. Additional amounts are available as guaranteed loans made by a financial institution.

ELIGIBILITY REQUIREMENTS: *Applicant Eligibility:* Must have produced, distributed, or sold a product in which there was a finding of toxicity from natural or unknown causes, making the product unfit for human consumption. Loans are available only where SBA has determined that such finding has resulted in economic injury to small business concerns. Requires such a determination in order to become operative.

APPLICATION AND AWARD PROCESS: *Preapplication Coordination:* Generally, preapplication interviews are held to determine eligibility to apply and to advise applicant generally on what assistance can be made available. *Application Procedure:* Applications are filed with the nearest SBA field office (see listing in catalog appendix) on SBA Form 5 provided for this purpose. Only one copy of the application need be filed.
Award Procedure: Applicant is notified of approval by authorization letter from district SBA office.

INFORMATION CONTACTS: *Regional or Local Office:* Field offices (region and district). *Headquarters Office:* Office of Disaster Operations, Small Business Administration, 1441 L St., N.W., Washington, DC 20416. Telephone: (202) 382-3175.

CANADIAN GOVERNMENTAL RESOURCES

For information on governmental resources available in Canada, contact the Director General, Emergency Planning Canada, 3rd Floor, Tower B, Lester B. Pearson Building, Ottawa, Ontario K1A 0W6. Telephone (416) 992-2727.

PRIVATE AND QUASI-PRIVATE RESOURCES

The primary resource in this category is the American National Red Cross. Though chartered by the United States Congress, the Red Cross is dependent upon private, rather than tax, funds for its work.

American National Red Cross

The American National Red Cross is required by its Congressional charter to undertake relief activities to mitigate suffering caused by disaster.

The Red Cross cooperates with all federal, state, and local government agencies and refers and receives clients according to the services to be rendered.

Local chapters may be entirely volunteer or have paid staff. A group of chapters form a division; some chapters and divisions have extensive rolling stock and equipment. The chapter or division has immediate action responsibility: for recruiting, training, and utilization of volunteers and for providing needed resources. Additional personnel and supplies are provided by one of the four area offices and national headquarters in Washington.

Red Cross Training Courses

1. American Red Cross—3065—Introduction to
   Disaster Services   1 hour
2. American Red Cross—3066—How the
   Red Cross Chapter Renders Emergency Assistance to
   Disaster Victims   1½ hours
3. American Red Cross—3067—How to Conduct
   Disaster Damage Assessment   3 hours
4. American Red Cross—3068—Disaster Feeding
   Operations   1 hour
5. American Red Cross—3072—Emergency
   Assistance to Families   8 hours
6. American Red Cross—3073—Additional Assistance
   to Families   24 hours
7. American Red Cross—3074—Shelter
   Management   6 hours
8. American Red Cross—3076—Providing Health
   Services in Disasters   6 hours
9. American Red Cross—Disaster Public
   Relations/Information Workshop   12 hours
10. American Red Cross—MultiMedia
    First Aid Course   8 hours
11. American Red Cross—Advanced
    First Aid Course   24 hours
12. American Camping Association—Campcrafter   16 hours
13. American Camping Association—Advanced
    Campcrafter   16 hours
14. Disaster Simulation   16 hours
15. Disaster Assistance Experience   16 hours
16. WIN Training   16 hours
17. Crisis Counseling Training   16 hours

These training courses are available from your nearest Red
Cross chapter.

WHEN DISASTERS STRIKES*

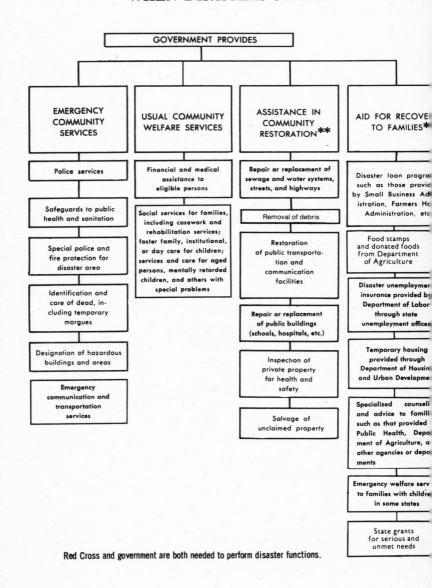

GOVERNMENT PROVIDES

EMERGENCY COMMUNITY SERVICES

- Police services
- Safeguards to public health and sanitation
- Special police and fire protection for disaster area
- Identification and care of dead, including temporary morgues
- Designation of hazardous buildings and areas
- Emergency communication and transportation services

USUAL COMMUNITY WELFARE SERVICES

- Financial and medical assistance to eligible persons
- Social services for families, including casework and rehabilitation services; foster family, institutional, or day care for children; services and care for aged persons, mentally retarded children, and others with special problems

ASSISTANCE IN COMMUNITY RESTORATION**

- Repair or replacement of sewage and water systems, streets, and highways
- Removal of debris
- Restoration of public transportation and communication facilities
- Repair or replacement of public buildings (schools, hospitals, etc.)
- Inspection of private property for health and safety
- Salvage of unclaimed property

AID FOR RECOVE TO FAMILIES*

- Disaster loan progra such as those provide by Small Business Ad istration, Farmers Ho Administration, etc
- Food stamps and donated foods from Department of Agriculture
- Disaster unemploymen insurance provided by Department of Labor through state unemployment office
- Temporary housing provided through Department of Housin and Urban Developme
- Specialized counseli and advice to famili such as that provided Public Health, Depa ment of Agriculture, a other agencies or depa ments
- Emergency welfare serv to families with childre in some states
- State grants for serious and unmet needs

Red Cross and government are both needed to perform disaster functions.

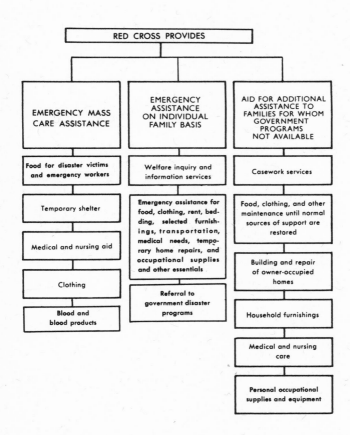

RED CROSS PROVIDES

EMERGENCY MASS CARE ASSISTANCE	EMERGENCY ASSISTANCE ON INDIVIDUAL FAMILY BASIS	AID FOR ADDITIONAL ASSISTANCE TO FAMILIES FOR WHOM GOVERNMENT PROGRAMS NOT AVAILABLE
Food for disaster victims and emergency workers	Welfare inquiry and information services	Casework services
Temporary shelter	Emergency assistance for food, clothing, rent, bedding, selected furnishings, transportation, medical needs, temporary home repairs, and occupational supplies and other essentials	Food, clothing, and other maintenance until normal sources of support are restored
Medical and nursing aid	Referral to government disaster programs	Building and repair of owner-occupied homes
Clothing		Household furnishings
Blood and blood products		Medical and nursing care
		Personal occupational supplies and equipment

° The chart shows how distinct and yet how closely related are the responsibilities of Red Cross and of government in natural disasters.
°° Some of these programs are activated only after a Presidential Declaration of a major disaster. Federal disaster assistance is coordinated by the Federal Disaster Assistance Administration of the Department of Housing and Urban Development.

Reprinted by permission from the American Red Cross leaflet, "Your Community Could Have a Disaster," December, 1977.

Red Cross Area Offices and Service Jurisdictions

National Headquarters
17th & D. Sts., N.W.
Washington, DC 20006

Eastern Area
615 North St. Asaph St.,
Alexandria, VA 22314

Connecticut
Delaware
District of Columbia
Indiana—Dearborn and Ohio Co., Franklin Co., and Switzerland
Co. chapters
Kentucky—Boone Co., Campbell Co., Kenton Co., and the
following chapters: Boyd Co., Greenup Co., Lewis Co., Bracken
Co., Grant Co., Gallatin Co., Mason Co., Owen Co., and
Pendleton Co.
Maine
Maryland
Massachusetts
New Hampshire
New Jersey
New York

Southeastern Area
1955 Monroe Dr., N.E.
Atlanta, GA 30324

Alabama
Arkansas (*except* Miller Co. and Little River Co.)
Florida
Georgia
Indiana—Clark Co., Crawford Co., Harrison Co., and New
Albany-Floyd Co. chapters
North Carolina—U.S. Coast Guard, Elizabeth City, and the
following chapters: Camden Co., Chowan Co., Currituck Co.,
Dare Co., Gates Co., Pasquotank Co., and Perquimans Co.
Ohio
Pennsylvania
Rhode Island
Vermont

Virginia (*except* Big Stone Gap, Bristol-Virginia-Tennessee,
  Buchana Co., Dickenson Co., Eastern Wise Co., Lee Co., Russell
  Co., and Scott Co. chapters
West Virginia

Kentucky (*except* Boone Co., Campbell Co., Kenton Co., and the
  following chapters: Boyd Co., Bracken Co., Daviess Co., Gallatin
  Co., Grant Co., Greenup Co., Hancock Co., Henderson Co.,
  Lewis Co., Mason Co., Owen Co., Pendleton Co., Sturgis, Union
  Co., and Webster Co.)
Louisiana
Mississippi
North Carolina (*except* U.S. Coast Guard, Elizabeth City, and the
  following chapters: Camden Co., Chowan Co., Currituck Co.,
  Dare Co., Gates Co., Pasquotank Co., and Perquimans Co.)

Midwestern Area
4050 Lindell Blvd.
St. Louis, MO 63108

Arkansas—Miller Co. and Little River Co.
Illinois
Indiana (*except* Clark Co., Crawford Co., Dearborn Co., Ohio Co.,
  Franklin Co., Harrison Co., New Albany-Floyd Co., and
  Switzerland Co. chapters)
Iowa
Kansas
Kentucky—Daviess Co., Hancock Co., Henderson Co., Sturgis,
  Union Co., and Webster Co. chapters

Western Area
1550 Sutter St.
San Francisco, CA 94101

Alaska
Arizona
California
Colorado
Idaho
Montana
Nevada
South Carolina
Tennessee

Virginia—Big Stone Gap, Bristol-Virginia-Tennessee, Buchanan Co., Dickenson Co., Eastern Wise Co., Lee Co., Russell Co., and Scott Co. chapters.
Michigan
Minnesota
Missouri
Nebraska
North Dakota
Oklahoma
South Dakota
Texas
Wisconsin
Wyoming—Crook Co., chapter and Weston Co.
New Mexico
Oregon
Utah
Washington
Wyoming (*except* Crook Co. chapter and Weston Co.)

Hawaii State Chapter

Insular Chapters:
    American Samoa Chapter
    Canal Zone Chapter
    Guam Chapter
    Puerto Rico Chapter
    Virgin Islands Chapter

Canadian Red Cross Society

The primary role for the provision of disaster relief assistance to victims of natural disasters in Canada has in the past been handled by the public authorities (municipal, provincial and federal) with nongovernmental agencies playing a relatively minor role.

Canadian Red Cross Society is not as heavily involved in providing assistance as the American National Red Cross is, although they do, upon request, assist disaster victims for the first 96 hours. These services include minimal shelter, food, clothing, and the like. Assistance is usually in the form of cash payment, if possible, which is recoverable in some cases from government authorities. The situation, however, is different in each of the ten divisions (which are analogous to provincial government jurisdictions). Separate working arrangements with the provincial authorities creates slight variations in programs across Canada.

National Commissioner
95 Wellesley Street, E.
Toronto, Canada M4Y 1H6

Division	Address
British Columbia-Yukon	4750 Oak Street Vancouver, B.C. V6H 2N9
Alberta-Northwest Territories	1504 First Street, S.E. Calgary, Alberta T2G 2J5
Saskatchewan	2571 Broad Street P.O. B. 1185 Regina, Saskatchewan
Manitoba	226 Osborne Street, North Winnipeg, Manitoba
Ontario	460 Jarvis Street Toronto, Ontario
Quebec	2170 Dorchester Blvd., West Montreal, P.Q. H3H 1R6
New Brunswick	Bayard Hill (Hospital Hill) P.O. B. 39 Saint John, New Brunswick
Nova Scotia	1940 Gottingen Street Halifax, N.S.

Prince Edward Island   62 Prince Street
                                    Charlottetown
                                    Prince Edward Island C1A 4R2

Newfoundland   55 Duckworth Street
                                    St. John's, Newfoundland

American Bar Association

The Young Lawyers Section of the American Bar Association has a national policy of providing assistance to low income persons and families needing legal services as a result of a major disaster. This policy is implemented through the Young Lawyers Section of state bar associations, and each state organization should have a person responsible for implementing and coordinating this service when it is needed.

National Headquarters
1155 East 60th Street
Chicago, IL 60637
(312) 947-4000

FOUNDATIONS

Private foundations and charitable trusts represent a resource for possible funding of a disaster recovery program. This source should be neither overestimated nor dismissed entirely.

Local corporation and family foundations with an interest in the affected community represent the best possibilities. Large or remote foundations cannot ordinarily be expected to respond to an appeal.

All foundations in the United States must file reports with the office of the State Attorney General in the state where they are chartered. These reports are public documents and may represent a good point of access to information about foundations in a particular city or state, if this information is not available in a more convenient form. Following is a listing of depositories of foundation annual reports and other documents which might also give leads to foundation resources in the United States.

Depositories of Foundational Annual Reports

Location	Geographical Coverage
The Foundation Center 888 Seventh Ave. New York, NY 10019	National
The Foundation Center 1001 Connecticut Ave., N.W. Washington, DC 20036	National
Donors' Forum 208 So. LaSalle St. Chicago, IL 60604	National

Alabama
Birmingham Public Library   Alabama
2020 Seventh Ave., North
Birmingham 35203

Arkansas
Little Rock Public Library   Arkansas
Reference Department
700 Louisiana St.
Little Rock 72201

California
University Research Library   Alaska, Arizona, California,
Reference Department   Colorado, Hawaii, Nevada,
University of California   Utah
Los Angeles 90024

San Francisco Public Library   Alaska, California, Colorado,
Business Branch   Hawaii, Idaho, Montana,
530 Kearny St.   Nevada, Oregon, Utah,
San Francisco 94108   Washington, Wyoming

Colorado
Denver Public Library   Colorado
Sociology Division
1357 Broadway
Denver 80203

Connecticut
Hartford Public Library   Connecticut, Massachusetts,
Reference Department   Rhode Island
500 Main St.
Hartford, 06103

Florida
Jacksonville Public Library   Florida
Business, Science, & Industry Dept.
122 North Ocean St.
Jacksonville 32202

Miami-Dade Public Library   Florida
Florida Collection
One Biscayne Blvd.
Miami 33132

Georgia
    Atlanta Public Library
    126 Carnegie Way, N.W.
    Atlanta 30303

Alabama, Florida, Georgia
Kentucky, Mississippi, North
Carolina, South Carolina,
Tennessee, Virginia

Hawaii
    Thomas Hale Hamilton Library
    Humanities & Social Sciences
    Reference
    2550 The Mall
    Honolulu 96809

California, Hawaii, Oregon,
Washington

Iowa
    Des Moines Public Library
    100 Locust St.
    Des Moines 40309

Iowa

Kansas
    Topeka Public Library
    Adult Services Department
    1515 W. Tenth St.
    Topeka 66604

Kansas

Kentucky
    Louisville Free Public Library
    Fourth & York Sts.
    Louisville 20203

Kentucky

Louisiana
    New Orleans Public Library
    Business & Science Division
    219 Loyola Ave.
    New Orleans 70140

Louisiana

Maine
    Center for Research
      & Advance Study
    University of Maine at
      Portland-Gorham
    246 Deering Ave.
    Portland 04102

Maine

Maryland
Enoch Pratt Free Library   Maryland
Social Science & History Dept.
400 Cathedral St.
Baltimore 21201

Massachusetts
Associated Foundation of   Connecticut, Maine,
   Greater Boston   Massachusetts, New
One Boston Place, Suite 948   Hampshire, Rhode Island,
Boston 02108   Vermont

Boston Public Library   Massachusetts
Copley Square
Boston 02117

Michigan
Henry Ford Centennial Library   Michigan
15301 Michigan Ave.
Dearborn 48126

Grand Rapids Public Library   Michigan
Sociology & Education Dept.
Library Plaza
Grand Rapids 49502

Minnesota
Minneapolis Public Library   Iowa, Minnesota, North
Sociology Dept.   Dakota, South Dakota
300 Nicollet Mall
Minneapolis 55401

Mississippi
Jackson Metropolitan Library   Mississippi
301 North State St.
Jackson 39201

Missouri
Kansas City Public Library   Kansas, Missouri
311 East 12th St.
Kansas City 64106

The Danforth Foundation Library   Iowa, Kansas, Missouri,
222 S. Central Ave.   Nebraska
St. Louis 63105

Nebraska
    Omaha Public Library   Nebraska
    1823 Harney St.
    Omaha 68102

New Hampshire
    The New Hampshire Charitable   New Hampshire
    One South St.   Fund
    Concord 03301

New Jersey
    New Jersey State Library   New Jersey
    Reference Section
    185 W. State St.
    Trenton 08625

New York
    New York State Library   New York
    State Education Dept.
    Education Building
    Albany 12224

    Buffalo & Erie Co. Public Library   New York
    Lafayette Square
    Buffalo 14203

    Levittown Public Library   New York
    Reference Department
    One Bluegrass Lane
    Levittown 11756

    Rochester Public Library   New York
    Business & Social Sciences Division
    115 South Ave.
    Rochester 14604

North Carolina
    William R. Perkins Library   North Carolina
    Duke University
    Durham 27706

Ohio
    The Cleveland Foundation   Michigan, Ohio,
    700 National City Bank Bldg.   Pennsylvania, West Virginia
    Cleveland 44114

Oklahoma
  Oklahoma City   Oklahoma
    Community Foundation
  1300 North Broadway
  Oklahoma City 73103

Oregon
  Library Association of Portland   Alaska, California, Hawaii,
  Education & Psychology Dept.   Oregon, Washington
  801 S.W. Tenth Ave.
  Portland 97205

Pennsylvania
  The Free Library of Philadelphia   Delaware, New Jersey,
  Logan Square   Pennsylvania
  Philadelphia 19103

  Hillman Library   Pennsylvania
  University of Pittsburgh
  Pittsburgh 15213

Rhode Island
  Providence Public Library   Rhode Island
  Reference Dept.
  150 Empire St.
  Providence 02903

South Carolina
  South Carolina State Library   South Carolina
  Reader Services Dept.
  1500 Senate St.
  Columbia 29211

Tennessee
  Memphis Public Library   Tennessee
  1850 Peabody Ave.
  Memphis 38104

Texas
  The Hogg Foundation for   Arkansas, Louisiana, New
    Mental Health   Mexico, Oklahoma, Texas
  The University of Texas
  Austin 78712

Dallas Public Library   Texas
History & Social Sciences Division
1954 Commerce St.
Dallas 75201

Utah
Salt Lake City Public Library   Utah
Information & Adult Services
209 East Fifth St.
Salt Lake City 84111

Vermont
State of Vermont Dept. of Libraries   New Hampshire, Vermont
Reference Services Unit
111 State St.
Montpelier 05602

Virginia
Richmond Public Library   Virginia
Business, Science & Technology
    Department
101 East Franklin St.
Richmond 23219

Washington
Seattle Public Library   Washington
1000 Fourth Ave.
Seattle 98104

West Virginia
Kanawha C. Public Library   West Virginia
123 Capitol St.
Charleston 25301

Wisconsin
Marquette Univ., Memorial Library   Illinois, Indiana, Iowa,
1415 W. Wisconsin Ave.   Michigan, Minnesota,
Milwaukee 53233   Ohio, Wisconsin

Wyoming
Laramie Co. Community   Wyoming
    College Library
1400 East College Dr.
Cheyenne 82001

Canadian Foundations

For information on private foundations in Canada, the best source is The Management and Fund Raising Center, 287 MacPherson Avenue, Toronto, Ontario M4V 1A4

CHURCH RESOURCES

Until very recently, church resources for responding to natural disasters in the United States and Canada have been quite limited, though church resources for overseas relief have been generous.

This directory of church resources indicates the kinds of assistance which can come from various religious organizations. One resource which is not listed here but which may provide assistance, is the state and/or local interchurch organization or council of churches. A list of such ecumenical agencies is available annually in the *Yearbook of American and Canadian Churches*, prepared by the Office of Research and Evaluation of the National Council of the Churches of Christ in the U.S.A., 475 Riverside Drive, New York NY 10027. The *Yearbook* is published and distributed by Abingdon Press.

Church World Service

CWS Domestic Disaster Coordinator
Box 188
New Windsor, MD 21776
(301) 635-6464

CWS Material Resources Director
475 Riverside Drive, Room 630
New York, NY 10027
(212) 870-2066

Church World Service, the cooperative relief and development agency of 29 U.S. Protestant and Orthodox communions, has since 1946 provided aid overseas, and since 1972 has responded to disasters in the United States. The CWS Committee on January 27, 1977, reconfirmed its previous action as follows:

VOLUNTEER ORGANIZATIONS
ACTIVE IN DISASTER RESOURCES

	Professional Staff	Trained Staff	Trained Volunteers	Untrained Staff	Untrained Volunteers
American National Red Cross	X	X	X	X	X
Ananda Marga (Amurt)	X	X	X	X	–
B'nai B'rith	X	–	–	–	X
Church of the Brethren	X	X	X	X	X
Christian Reformed World Relief	X	X	X	X	X
Church World Service	X	X	X	–	–
Good Will Industries	X	X	X	X	X
Lutheran Church of America	X	–	–	–	X
Mennonite Disaster Service	X	X	X	–	X
National Catholic Dis. Relief Comm.	X	X	X	X	X
National Catholic Conference and Catholic Charities	X	X	X	X	X
The Salvation Army	X	X	X	X	X
Seventh-Day Adventists	X	X	X	X	X
Southern Baptist Convention	X	X	X	X	X
Society of St. Vincent de Paul	X	X	X	X	X
United Methodist Church Comm.	X	X	X	X	X
Volunteers of America	X	X	X	X	X

Note:

A. Congressional Mandate. If no other resource Red Cross will meet needs.

B. Expertise in establishing inter-faith organization.

C. Bulk food distribution, warehousing ready supplies.

Buses	Station Wagons	Rescue Equipment	Communication Equipment	Clothing	Bedding	Used Furniture	Materials for Rebuilding Homes	Collection and Dist. of Donated Goods Other Than Clothing	Collection, Sorting, Sizing, of Used Clothing	Cleaning Debris from Private Property	Cleaning Homes	Free Labor to Repair or Rebuild Homes	Welfare Inquiry Service	Registration and Information Service	Counseling Service	Capability to Handle Crisis Intervention and Long-term Recovery	Training	Financial Assistance	Comments
X	X	X	X	X	X	–	X	–	–	–	–	–	X	X	X	–	X	X	A
–	–	–	X	X	X	X	–	X	X	–	–	–	X	X	X	–	X	X	
–	–	–	–	–	–	–	–	X	X	X	X	–	–	–	–	–	–	–	
–	–	–	–	–	–	–	–	–	–	X	X	X	–	X	–	–	–	–	B
X	X	–	X	X	X	X	X	X	X	X	X	X	X	X	X	X	X	X	B
–	–	–	–	X	X	–	–	–	–	–	–	–	–	–	–	–	–	X	H
–	X	X	X	–	–	–	–	–	–	–	–	–	–	–	–	–	X	X	
–	–	–	–	X	X	–	–	–	–	–	–	–	X	X	X	X	X	X	H
–	–	–	–	–	–	–	–	–	–	X	X	X	–	–	–	–	–	–	B
–	–	–	–	X	X	X	–	–	–	–	–	–	–	–	X	X	–	X	H
–	–	–	–	X	X	X	–	–	–	–	–	–	–	–	X	X	–	X	H
X	X	–	X	X	X	X	X	X	X	–	–	–	X	X	X	X	X	X	C
X	X	X	X	X	X	X	X	X	X	X	X	X	X	X	X	–	X	X	D
X	–	–	X	X	X	–	–	X	X	X	X	X	X	X	X	X	X	X	E
X	X	X	–	–	X	X	–	X	X	X	X	X	X	X	X	X	X	X	F
X	X	–	–	X	X	X	X	X	X	X	X	X	–	X	X	–	X	X	H
X	X	X	X	X	X	X	X	X	X	X	X	X	X	X	X	X	X	X	G

D. Private mobile homes available for major disasters.

E. $100,000 revolving fund and more if needed.

F. Maybe only in one or a few larger councils

G. Ambulances and air transporation and rescue.

H. Revolving Funds from $50,000 to 100,000 available.

(1) That CWS, on behalf of its member denominations and related agencies, shall initiate a response within its capabilities to natural disasters or severe community damage caused by human events in the USA and shall inform appropriate national and regional conciliar units of its action and response.

(2) That a CWS Domestic Disaster Coordinator be appointed.

Based on experience, the CWS response has taken the form of making available, on request by an interchurch group in a disaster area, a trained CWS resource person for a short period of time to help them organize to respond, to make limited funds and material aid available, and to help the local church groups find sources of further funding or other assistance. It is a short-term and catalytic role.

CWS will hold seminars to alert and train regional and local church leaders to opportunities for service and some of the inherent problems.

Church World Service Material Resources. Church World Service, through its ongoing clothing program, has blankets and clothing properly baled and sorted by type. Request may be made to the CWS Disaster Coordinator. CWS will usually respond to each request *when* they are made by a Church Response Group or similar interchurch group *and when* assured it is not available from nearby churches or from the Red Cross, Salvation Army, and the like, and that it will be distributed according to need, without regard for church membership.

Church World Service does not maintain emergency food supplies nor does it supply items for public health or medical use. However, on occasion, CWS will supply water purification tablets for use in rural areas but only after the church response assures CWS that it has *written* approval from public health authorities.

Funding. The church response organization needs funds immediately to meet unmet needs of the disaster victims.

Local churches, agencies, or individuals may be able to provide or advance limited funds, and those in nearby cities may supplement these. Contributions may be solicited as time permits. In most cases, if a local or regional body solicits or receives contributions for the disaster, they would be sent directly to the church response treasurer.

Financial Resources. Grants and loans should be made to meet immediate unmet needs without jeopardizing the victims' dignity nor adversely affecting opportunity to be assisted from other resources. Church World Service is not a major source of funding in a disaster. Limited funds may be available to meet unmet needs of the victim, or to provide initial funding to enable the church response to become operative.

CWS may receive funding requests based on the church response group's budget. The budget should reflect a realistic appraisal of unmet needs, program, and ability of the church response group to provide necessary services. In budget preparation, keep in mind that limited resources are available to the denominations, boards, and agencies. Income should determine program rather than anticipated financial support. These requests are routed to national denominations by the CWS Executive Director. Denominations there decide individually the amount each will contribute to that budget.

Denominational support in answer to the CWS Executive Director's situation report or disaster memorandum will not necessarily be transmitted to CWS. In some cases the denominational funds from a national office will flow through a conference, district, presbytery, or other judicatory, which then should channel the funds, when so designated, to the church response group. Funds received by CWS in support of the request from the church response organization are immediately transmitted. It is necessary that reports be received on the responsible use of these monies so that future requests will be supported by the denominations, boards, and agencies.

Rebuilding or restoring church property normally is a denominational activity and does not become part of the church response organization program.

Christian Reformed Church

Director
2850 Kalamazoo Avenue, S.E.
Grand Rapids, MI 49508
(616) 241-1691

CRWRC has a corps of trained volunteers ready to move on 24-hour notice into any disaster area in the United States or Canada. Volunteers are trained particularly in person-to-person services for the elderly, the retarded, the disabled, and one-parent families. Emphasis is upon helping individuals find the assistance offered by governments and the Red Cross, and on offering spiritual counsel, personal concern, and a listening ear.

CRWRC also sends material, financial, and volunteer aid into disaster areas. During emergencies in areas where the Christian Reformed Church is not present,

CRWRC often channels disaster aid through other church groups and mission organizations.

CRWRC maintains a warehouse for storage of clothing, blankets, and other items. CRWRC staff and groups with which they cooperate may order these materials when needed for emergency aid.

Church of the Brethren Disaster Response

Director
P.O. Box 188
New Windsor, MD 21776
(301) 635-6464

The purpose of the Church of the Brethren Disaster Response (Brethren Service) is to minister to the needs of individuals following natural or man-made disasters. The primary Brethren disaster response has been to provide volunteers for the cleaning up process and rebuilding homes, as well as some financial support.

Volunteers working for short periods of time assist in the physical, emotional, and spiritual recovery following the impact of the disaster. Skilled and semiskilled volunteers are utilized for the long-term rebuilding and reconstruction efforts.

Although the Church of the Brethren is recognized for cleanup, repair, and rebuilding, personnel may be available for transportation, as caseworkers, blood donors, medical workers, and for other needs that can be served by volunteers.

For long-scale disasters, the local coordinator or district coordinator generally will survey the disaster site or confer with others on the scene. Following a consultation with the national staff, a call will be issued for volunteers.

Through the disaster network, the request for volunteers is generally directed to a geographical area closest to the disaster, with specific requests to local congregations for persons or equipment as needed. Volunteers normally provide their own transportation. Local churches, other voluntary agencies, private homes, or other housing arrangements may be utilized to provide housing for the volunteers. Generally, the cost of food and housing for the volunteers is borne by denominational disaster funds, thus incurring no cost to the community nor to the disaster victims.

Mennonite Disaster Service

National Director
Mennonite Disaster Service
21 South 12th St.
Akron, PA 17501
(717) 859-1151

MDS Units by Regions

Region I
1. Alabama & Northwest Florida
2. Central & South Florida
3. Cumberland Valley, Pennsylvania
4. Delmarva Peninsula
5. Eastern Pennsylvania
6. Georgia
7. Lancaster Area, Pennsylvania
8. New England States
9. New York City
10. North Carolina & Eastern Tennessee
11. Northern New York
12. Penn-York
13. Puerto Rico & Virgin Islands
14. Shenandoah Valley, Virginia
15. South Carolina
16. Tidewater, Virginia
17. Western New York
18. Western Pennsylvania & Maryland

Region II
1. Eastern Ohio
2. Illinois
3. Indiana & Lower Michigan
4. Kentucky & Tennessee
5. Michigan
6. Mississippi-Louisiana
7. Western Ohio
8. Wisconsin

Region III
1. Arkansas
2. Colorado
3. Eastern Montana
4. Iowa
5. Kansas
6. Minnesota
7. Missouri
8. Nebraska
9. New Mexico
10. North Dakota
11. Northern Minnesota
12. Oklahoma
13. South Dakota
14. South Texas
15. Western Montana

Region IV
1. Arizona
2. California
3. Eastern Washington

3. Eastern Washington
4. Hawaii
5. Idaho
6. Oregon
7. Western Washington

Region V
1. Alberta
2. Borderland (includes Western Ontario and Lakes Region, Minnesota)
3. British Columbia
4. Manitoba
5. Atlantic
6. Ontario
7. Saskatchewan

Transnational
1. Belize
2. Dominican Republic
3. Honduras

The purpose of Mennonite Disaster Service is to assist individuals and communities in repair and rehabilitation work following a disaster. Through Mennonite Disaster Service assistance is available for—

(1) General, immediate cleanup and restoration of disaster locations, including at times prevention, warning, evacuation, and search and rescue operations;

(2) Temporary repairs to damaged homes so that they can be reoccupied; and

(3) Reconstruction and rehabilitation of residences and vital building facilities in an affected community.

Any disaster victim or community which has sustained damage because of a major disaster is eligible for assistance.

Mennonite Disaster Service Organizational Chart

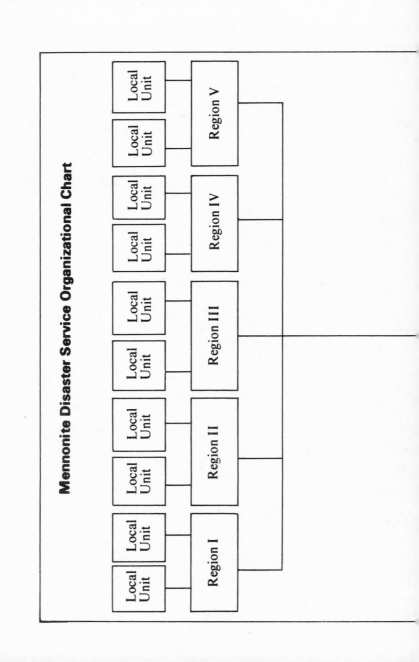

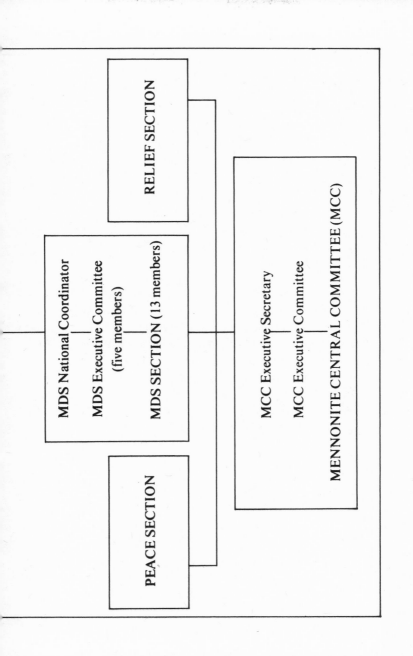

RELIEF SECTION

PEACE SECTION

MDS National Coordinator

MDS Executive Committee
(five members)

MDS SECTION (13 members)

MCC Executive Secretary

MCC Executive Committee

MENNONITE CENTRAL COMMITTEE (MCC)

National Catholic Disaster Relief Committee

1846 Connecticut Ave., N.W.
Washington, DC 20036
(202) 785-2757

The National Catholic Disaster Relief Committee is attached for administrative purposes to the National Conference of Catholic Charities, which supplies staff support and assistance to the committee. When a major disaster strikes anywhere in the United States, committee staff contacts the bishop of the affected diocese(s) and the local office of Catholic Charities. An assessment is made of the extent of need.

If outside assistance is needed, consultants may go to the affected area to advise the local church authorities. Volunteers are recruited as needed, and some immediate financial assistance may be made available from the committee's small emergency fund. If the disaster is of a major proportion, the committee may launch a national appeal through the local diocese.

The committee itself consists of seventeen persons who are representatives of various sections of the United States and a variety of Catholic activities.

Salvation Army Emergency Disaster Service

The Salvation Army is a religious and charitable movement, finding its expression in a desire to alleviate human distress wherever found. It is not primarily an emergency disaster relief organization, but by tradition and inclination usually finds itself serving at the point of greatest need, during the emergency period of a disaster.

The Salvation Army is an international movement organized to serve nationwide. Its primary emergency service is financed by available resources and donations. Long-range service, if required, is funded by special appeals.

The network of varied programs for human betterment is so geared as to be readily available for emergencies. Trained personnel is ready to give essential relief where needed. These services are rendered by formal agreement or as need requires.

Salvation Army emergency service may include:

(1) Evacuation
(2) Emergency feeding (mass and individual)
(3) Food distribution
(4) Shelter (mass and individual)
(5) Clothing distribution
(6) Counseling (spiritual ministry)
(7) Personal inquiry services (missing persons)
(8) Welfare, family rehabilitation
   a. Casework
   b. Furniture and bedding
   c. Household needs
(9) Services to disaster workers

Services outlined are to be rendered as needed and as resources are available. Caution should be exercised to avoid any attempt to cover needs which must be met through other means.

Other U.S. Church Disaster Relief Agencies

Christian Church (Disciples of Christ)
Committee on the Week of Compassion Fund
Box 1986
22 S. Downey Avenue
Indianapolis, IN 46206
(317) 353-1491

The Episcopal Church
Presiding Bishop's Fund for World Relief
815 Second Avenue
New York, NY 10017
(212) 867-8400

Presbyterian Church in the U.S.
Department of Health and Welfare
341 Ponce de Leon Avenue, N.E.
Atlanta, GA 30308
(404) 875-8921

Reformed Church in America
General Program Council
475 Riverside Drive
New York, NY 10027

United Methodist Church
United Methodist Committee on Relief
Board of Global Ministries
475 Riverside Drive, Rm. 1470
New York, NY 10027
(212) 749-0700

Every United Methodist Conference has been asked to designate a disaster response coordinator.

United Presbyterian Church, U.S.A.
Office of World Relief and Emergency Services
The Program Agency
475 Riverside Drive
New York, NY 10027
(212) 870-3041

Southern Baptist Convention
Brotherhood Commission
1548 Poplar Avenue
Memphis, TN 38104

Some State Baptist Conventions have been very active and well-equipped disaster response teams—Texas and Oklahoma, for example. In other areas, the emphasis is entirely upon raising funds for repair of Southern Baptist church-owned property.

Friend's Disaster Service
Coordinator
241 Keenan Road
Peninsula, OH 44264
(216) 653-6814

General Conference of Seventh-Day Adventists
6840 Eastern Avenue, N.W.
Washington, DC 20012
(202) 723-0800

Each conference (approximately state lines) has a Director of Lay Activities and Community Services who is responsible for disaster response within the area of the conference.

Canadian Church Resources

Church Action for Emergency Aid
The Canadian Council of Churches
40 St. Clair Avenue, E.
Toronto, Ontario M4T 1M9

This is the facility through which several Canadian churches may act together quickly in responding to appeals for emergency aid. Participants are Anglican, Baptist, Lutheran, Presbyterian, Roman Catholic, and United Church of Canada.

Christian Reformed Church World Relief Committee
178 Alway Road
P.O. Box 235
Grimsby, Ontario L3M 4G3

Mennonite Central Committee (Canada)
201-1483 Pembina Highway
Winnipeg, Manitoba R3T 2C8

All relief projects are administered by Mennonite Disaster Service, 21 South 12th Street, Akron, PA 17501 (U.S.A.). MCC (Canada) raises funds and recruits volunteers for participation in projects. (See MDS units list, pp. 160-161)

Religious Society of Friends, Canadian Yearly Meeting
60 Lowther Avenue
Toronto, Ontario M5R 1C7

The Salvation Army in Canada
20 Albert St.
Toronto, Ontario M5G 1A6

APPENDIX

Kentucky Interchurch Disaster Recovery Program (KIDRP)

Job Profile: Program Director

A director for the statewide program is needed as a full-time employee for up to two years. This should be a person with administrative and organizational skills. A strong Christian commitment and appreciation for the uniqueness of the church's role in society is essential. This person must be sensitive to the relational structures of the churches and of local communities, and must be aware of the special problems and needs of the people within the communities to be served.

The director is employed by and responsible to the Disaster Ministries Committee of Kentucky Council of Churches. His/her responsibility is seen as being in the following areas: administration, advocacy, program supervision, public information, supervision of program staff, and consultant/resource person to local interchurch disaster organizations.

Advocacy: The program director will act as advocate with local, state, and federal officials on behalf of flood victims generally and of individual clients and with special problems relating to disaster assistance programs. In local situations, the director will work with local area advisory groups.

Administration: Administrative supervision shall be provided to the program director by the Executive Director of Kentucky Council of Churches. Program supervision shall be provided by the Disaster Ministries Committee. The program director shall make monthly administrative reports, including regular financial reports, to the Executive Director. He/she shall report monthly to the Disaster Ministries Committee. He/she shall be responsible for employment of other staff persons with the approval of the committee. He/she shall see that the office of KIDRP is efficiently operated and maintained at the office of Kentucky Council of Churches, Lexington.

Program Supervision: The director shall provide supervision of the Kentucky Interchurch Disaster Recovery Program in accordance with the program and goals set forth by the committee.

Public Information: The director shall be responsible to keep all media aware of KIDRP progress in the affected areas through periodical news releases and other methods.

Staff Supervision: The director shall be responsible for supervision of all program staff. He/she shall be responsible for employment of program staff upon approval by the committee, and he/she shall coordinate volunteer staff.

Resourcing and Consultation: The director shall be the primary resource person and consultant to the area advisory groups and existing local interchurch or interfaith recovery groups. He/she shall supervise the organization of area advisory groups where these do not exist and maintain a working relationship with these groups.

In fulfilling all of his/her responsibilities, the program director shall have the full support of the Disaster Ministries Committee. He/she shall receive a compensation package totalling $15,000 per year plus FICA, and workman's compensation insurance. In the event that moving costs are necessitated by action of the committee, moving costs shall be paid. All necessary job related travel costs shall be paid or reimbursed.

(In the event that the person employed is a clergyperson, the compensation package shall include salary, housing allowance and denominational retirement program costs.)

John C. Bush is Executive Director of the Kentucky Council of Churches with offices at Lexington. His responsibilities have included an active disaster response ministry in five of the past six years.

From 1968 to 1973 he was Executive Director of the Interchurch Coordinating Council of West Central Missouri. He served as pastor of the Americus United Presbyterian Church, Americus, Kansas (1963-1966), and on the pastoral staff of Grand River Parish, Urich, Missouri (1967-1970).

The author received his Doctor of Ministry degree from San Francisco Theological Seminary, San Anselmo, California; has done graduate work at the University of Missouri School of Regional and Community Affairs; holds the Master of Divinity degree from Midwestern Baptist Theological Seminary, Kansas City, Missouri;

and completed his BA degree at Samford University, Birmingham, Alabama.

His articles have appeared in *Christian Century, Church Educator, Today, Lexington Newsmagazine, Social Action Review, Church Administration, Church Management,* and other publications.

Dr. Bush is on the board of directors of the Lexington Chapter of the National Conference for Christians and Jews and he is a member of the Citizens Advisory Council for Kentucky Educational Television.

John and Sara (Fulton) Bush are active in the Second Presbyterian Church, Lexington. They are the parents of Michael David and Janet Lucille.